Shattered

to the Core

W9-BPN-032

HOW I MADE PEACE WITH MY PAST
AND RECLAIMED MY FUTURE

by Valerie J. Walsh

CORE
PRESS

Copyright © 2022 by Valerie J. Walsh
All rights reserved. No part of this book may be used or reproduced in any manner whatsoever without written permission except in the case of brief quotations embodied in critical articles or reviews.

Published by CORE PRESS

Printed in the United States of America
10 9 8 7 6 5 4 3 2 1

paperback ISBN: 978-1-7379571-2-6
e-book ISBN: 978-1-7379571-3-3

Produced by GMK Writing and Editing, Inc.
Managing Editor: Katie Benoit
Copyedited by Randy Ladenheim-Gil and Proofread by Katie Sharp
Text design and composition by Libby Kingsbury and Sue Murray
Cover design by Libby Kingsbury
Printed by IngramSpark

Author's Note: In writing this book, I relied on my memory, years of journaling, interviewing family members and researching facts where I could. Names of some of the individuals who appear in my memoir have been changed.

Visit the author at www.valeriejwalsh.com

Connect with Valerie on:
Instagram: @valeriejwalshauthor
Facebook: @corefitnessmethod

"No one can pull you up very high—you lose your grip on the rope. But on your own two feet you can climb mountains."

—Louis Brandeis

For my mother...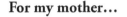

Everything you've taught me has a place in my heart,
Memories reflected on; proves we are never apart.
Your spirit is soaring and lifting me too,
Giving me strength, and I know that it's you.
All of my life you have done that for me,
Taking my burdens, so that I may be free.
Rest peacefully mother, knowing I am there,
Living my life, lighter than air.

—Valerie Walsh

For the 280 million people in the world who suffer with depression and other mental illnesses. There is hope, there is help. Find someone you can talk to. I promise you are not a burden. Please believe me when I say so, it's because I know so.

Acknowledgments

To my children, Bailey and Collin: May you always know it is okay to not feel okay, and when you feel this way, ask for help early on, the same way you would if you had a cold. Remember to keep your standards high and expectations low...*don't worry, you'll figure out what I mean by that someday!* Remain curious, kind, and coachable. Remember, strong teams learn, love, and win...together. May you find your CORE Team of Peeps in life and value that fellowship. Also, don't take yourself too seriously...laugh, like...a lot! Find people, places, and things that will help you do just that. Above all, know that I love you both, from deep inside my mama CORE.

To my sister, Monica: My Irish twin. Thank you for loving me enough to provide the support and blessing to write this book about our mother. The respect you have shown me to go down this road, even when it is a very different one than you have taken, is everything to me. I love you. You and I, since we were little kids, have this unspoken bond, but not anymore because I just wrote about it, ha! Just you wait 'til you read it! It's *all* coming out now. Kidding...you are one of my ultimate CORE Peeps, from the beginning.

To my husband, Brian: Thank you for loving me just the way I am. For allowing me to try new things and quietly supporting me. You and I have endured more than most married couples do in a lifetime together. I love you, always. Thank you for our beautiful children, who are so much like us...crap! Nah, we did good, baby.

They are hardworking, kindhearted, empathetic, smart, talented, funny peeps. I am so proud of the family we have created together.

To my CORE Peeps: I am blessed enough to have so many of you in my life, so I will not name you all individually. I hope I have taken the time to show each of you just how important you are to me; therefore you do not have to question whether this acknowledgment is meant for you…*Hint:* It is. I love you all. Thank you all for lifting me up and allowing me to do the same. A nonnegotiable in life, have strong CORE Peeps around, thank you for being mine.

To my aunt Donna: Thank you for being an extension of my beautiful, loving mother. When I am around you, I feel her energy, and I am so grateful for that. You are stronger than you know, and also one of the kindest. I love you. You were a huge part in the breakthrough of getting this book actually finished because you helped me to know who my mother was as a young woman. Thank you for having the courage to walk down that path with me.

To Trish: You take images of people in a way that captures exactly who they are. I wish I could take a picture of your beautiful soul; it would be the most magnificent image of all. You are light, thank you.

To Sasha: Thank you for always being by my side, literally, smothering me with support during this entire journey. By my side, as I wrote, cried, and laughed my way through this. You are my best friend.

To Elizabeth Copps: Thank you for taking on this project from the very beginning. You were the first person in the literary world who believed that my story deserved to be told and guided me to dig deeper. Thank you for going above and beyond line editing, to get me to where I needed to go.

Gary Krebs and Team: Thank you for responding to my email in the first place. I am so grateful to have connected with GMK Writing and Editing, Inc., including your colleagues, Katie Benoit Cardoso, Randy Ladenheim-Gil, and the very talented designer, Libby Kingsbury. Your combined expertise and direction were invaluable to me. It has been such and honor and privilege to work with each of you.

Contents

Introduction

Why do all the good ones have to go before us? That was a question my grandmother asked me shortly after my mother passed away. My grandmother was eighty-six and about to lay her fifty-nine-year-old daughter to rest, a horror no mother should have to face. She was heartbroken at the fact that her daughter had gone to sleep never to wake again. What my grandmother didn't know was that my mother had died by suicide.

I do not know why all the good ones have to go before us, but what I do know is that somewhere deep inside our core, it is ingrained in us to want our mothers to be a part of our lives in significant times. Times of happiness and sadness, and it is usually our mothers we turn to when we are afraid.

Which is where I found myself when I began journaling, writing the notes that would turn into this memoir.

I didn't know I was writing my memoir at the time; I just knew I had to put my thoughts and feelings somewhere, and paper was where they landed.

It took perspective—seven years' worth, to be exact—for me to piece those notes into *Shattered to the Core.* In those years, my mother's suicide provided me with the wake-up call I needed to stop living my life in fear and angst. To stop searching for signs that she was at peace and to turn that energy into finding my own.

I wrote this book with the purpose of sharing my story with others who may be struggling with mental illness and addiction. To give depression a face.

What does depression look like? It looks like the familiar faces of those around us, likely the ones we would never expect. Our colleagues, our coaches, our family members, our leaders. Some of the strongest people you know may be battling inside, putting on a brave front for the sake of others, as my sweet mother did.

My purpose with this book is to shatter the expectations of what depression looks like. To give hope to my readers that there are ways you can live a happy, fulfilling, and peaceful life, even if you are prone to mental illness.

I want to normalize the conversations surrounding mental illness, just like we talk about other sicknesses.

I want people who are struggling to feel comfortable enough to reach out to a friend, a colleague, anyone, and be able to say, "Hey, I am not doing okay. I am having a hard time and need some help" with the same comfort level they would have asking for help if they were sick with a cold.

I want my readers to know that with every fear, that voice within us can still our troubled minds. For me, that voice is God, and many times in my life, God has worked through others. I just needed the willingness to listen.

My hope is that we may all have the willingness, and when we don't, to allow our tribe of warriors to step in to help.

I am an intelligent person; I know what stress can do to someone. Hell, it is what I preach! Routine stressors such as work, managing a household, and daily responsibilities are *not* the type of stress I am referring to. No, the type of stress I am talking about here is trauma. The type of trauma that rocks your world, penetrating you to the core so hard you'd do anything to shield your face from the reality of what feels like it's literally eating away at your insides.

For over twenty years I was a personal trainer, a running coach, and a yoga and group fitness instructor. Physical fitness was not only my profession, it was also my passion.

"Exercise helps to reduce stress, so be sure to make it a priority in your life."

I've always had *that* part down, but no one likes a preacher, not even me. Maybe that was why I had a hard time heeding my own advice.

In the spring of 2013, stress, fueled by deep trauma, threatened to overwhelm me: My mother took her life and, six short months later, I would make the decision to cut off my breasts to save my own.

This is my story. It is a story about mental illness and addiction. About pain and loss. But it's a story packed with hope and healing as well. Grief is not a one-size-fits-all model. But what I discovered in the months and years after my sorrow is that it is much easier to recover from the physical scars than the emotional ones.

On the surface, intergenerational trauma can feel impossible to combat. Emotional scars become rooted deep inside one's soul; they extend themselves so far down, they seem bottomless. But if there is no end, maybe the only choice is to find a new beginning.

ONE

Floating—May 30, 2013

*"The spiritual journey is the unlearning of fear
and the acceptance of love."*

~Marianne Williamson

"Mom, Mom? Pick up your phone. I've been trying you since yesterday. Please pick up, Mom, I just want to be sure you're okay. If you don't call me back, I'm going to have to have someone stop by to check on you…I'm getting worried."

The last conversation I had with my mother the day before hadn't gone very well. She was angry, which was unlike her. My mother had a lifetime of battling depression and anxiety, although she never admitted it. But I knew, even when she tried her best to cover it up. Most times, she hid it by overcompensating. My mother crafted the art of diversion. Turning the focus off her and on to anything else was one of the many tricks she used to hide her suffering. She was also an incredibly generous person. Generous in the time she would give to anyone who needed a listening ear. And she was a talented seamstress who could sew a dress from any JCPenney pattern, which she did for my sister and me when we were young. Or knit a beautiful baby blanket for my babies, as well as many blankets, scarves, and countless gifts for anyone who was lucky enough to know her. However, in that last conversation there was a distinct difference in her voice. When she spoke, she unleashed venom from her tongue. She sounded disgusted with me, with everything.

"I wish I could get there with the kids this Memorial Day weekend, but they're both marching in the parade here in Connecticut, and we can't miss that. I promise this summer we will come a few times, not just for the NY State Fair Days weekend, okay?" I tried my best to reassure my mother.

"Whatever, Valerie. No one visits me anymore, and I can't go anywhere. I fucking hate this. It is so hard to go anywhere on oxygen, and no one wants to deal with taking me places. I'm done. I'm just done. I want to go….I want to be with my brother and my father!"

She was referring to my uncle Bill, who died at the age of thirty-seven from pneumococcal pneumonia in February 2000, thirteen years before. He was my mother's younger brother. This was the first time I had ever heard her admit she didn't want to live anymore, and I never thought she would actually go through with any plans she might have to kill herself.

My whole life I witnessed her survival. She was a warrior to me. A woman who constantly weathered the many storms that seemed so relentless to her. Yet, somehow, she always managed to come out on the other side. Surely she would ride out this wave of depression too?

She continued to cry to me about how difficult everything was for her, especially being tethered to oxygen.

My mother's health took a rapid decline in the fall of 2005, when she fell outside my home. She was there to help me after I gave birth to my second child, my son Collin. She had come to help with my daughter Bailey, who was five at the time. Mom went outside to get something for me and, in doing so, fell and severely broke both ankles. Her recovery was long and very painful. My mother began to slowly put on weight and take more pills to relieve the chronic pain she was in. The pills, mixed with her ongoing alcohol addiction, were a recipe for disaster. A year after her fall, at the age of fifty-five, she was diagnosed with pulmonary hypertension and COPD and placed on supplemental oxygen. It was a horrible way to live. She hated being on it and was constantly nervous that someone she knew would see her that way. Shortly after her diagnosis, she moved out of Connecticut and back to Syracuse, New York, the city where she raised my sister and me. It was there that she was hoping for another fresh start. Instead, she began to isolate and self-medicate more.

My sister Monica lived thirty minutes away from our mother, just outside of Syracuse. Now, I didn't want to concern her with the fact that I couldn't reach our mom. I knew she was at work, and besides, she had no clue how worried I really was. I didn't tell Monica about the dark exchange I had with Mom over the phone the day before. She had her own concerns, and I didn't want to add to them unnecessarily. Instead, I decided to wait until lunchtime to alert her if I still hadn't reached our mom by then.

Knowing I'd left demanding words for my mom to call me back, I decided to return to my spring training; I was preparing for my first-ever triathlon. *Besides,* I thought, *it was pretty early still...she just may be sleeping.*

It was the end of May in New Milford, Connecticut, and although the water temperature of Candlewood Lake wasn't exactly welcoming, I had to get my training in. I'm anything but a good swimmer, but I've always loved to bike and to run. Swimming...I'd always left that to the fish.

I remember lying in the lake that morning, floating, to catch my breath. Feeling weightless, supported by the cool water beneath my skin. Soaking in the warmth of the sun that framed the parts of my body exposed on the surface.

I remember the moment when the sun became brighter, and later thinking it was as if it was the exact moment my mother's soul left her body to pass through the atmosphere and into the heavens.

The promised visit to my mother would never happen. She died by suicide on Thursday, May 30, 2013.

Ironically, from that day on, just like my mother had showed me how, I did what I had to do; I went into survival mode. Life also did what it tends to do; it went on with no regard for the storm I was barely weathering. And mine—well, my life was a shitstorm of events that happened way too quickly, not allowing me any chance to properly mourn the loss of my mom, to truly grieve her, let alone process what she had done.

What she had done...

She took an entire bottle of pills and never woke up. Was it intentional? Or was she just looking for a brief, sweet release? Maybe she wanted to sleep for a little while, not thinking it would *really* happen?

I know how tired she was; the discourse of that final phone call replayed in my head, over and over. The promise I made to her: "Just look forward to this summer, Mom. I will be coming with the kids then."

She wouldn't make it to summer. She was too tired to fight any longer. Tired of combating her own mental illness. An illness never properly treated or diagnosed as she tried so hard to do it all, all her life, including self-medicate.

So, there she left me, floating on the surface of the lake, with one final kiss from the sunlight upon my face. My mother was gone, and I didn't know how to cope without knowing how she got to such a place of sheer desperation.

TWO

Like Mother, Like Daughter

*"The more a daughter knows the details of her mother's life,
the stronger the daughter."*

~Anita Diamant

My mother was very young when she had my sister and me. In the spring of her senior year of high school, she discovered she was pregnant. She and my biological father were very much in love, so they decided to marry on July 15, 1972. They moved into an attic apartment above my biological father's parents' house. The apartment consisted of one bedroom, a bathroom, a kitchenette, and a small living room. Then, on December 3, 1972, they welcomed a beautiful baby girl, my sister Monica. Only three months later, my mother would discover she was once again pregnant, with me. Barely twenty years old and already the mother of two, her Irish twins, at only eleven months apart.

My mother and father stayed in that small apartment rent-free, but it came at a cost: my mother's privacy and energy. The only entrance into their place was through her in-laws' house, making it nearly impossible to have any social life. With the looming reminder of being able to live there as something of a favor, she was also asked to do many chores around the house to help out, on top of raising two babies. She cooked, cleaned, and sewed, leaving her feeling like a real-life Cinderella.

They lived in that apartment for two years, until they realized they needed to try life on their own and moved us in and out of a few crummy apartments that my mother always had the knack for making as beautiful as she could while on welfare. The final place we all lived together was Franklin Park Apartments in East Syracuse, New York. There, things began to become dangerous. By then, my biological father had developed a pretty strong love of alcohol and gambling.

One night, my mother was alone with my sister and me, approximately two and three years old by then, when she heard very loud knocking on the door. These apartments were not in the safest area, making her cautious whenever someone came to the door, but this time, *she knew something was wrong.* The violent banging continued until my mother had no choice but to let them in or they were going to force their way. When she opened the door, there stood two thugs, holding onto our car seats.

"Take your seats, we're taking your car, get the keys, *now!*" the thugs demanded. "Tell your husband we'll be back for more."

My father was in over his head in gambling debts he had no means of paying off, putting his family in grave danger. These men meant business, and my mother had the good sense to finally say, "Enough."

Their marriage had lasted about three years, and for reasons that remained unclear to me my entire life, his relationship with us was also over. Perhaps his demons prevented him from being in our lives. Or maybe there were other reasons that were never made known to me. I discovered letters in my mother's hope chest after her death, when going through her things, from her grandmother, *my great-grandmother.* Letters she had written when I was born, congratulating her and letting her know how happy she was that my mother had found herself a "good man." *Those were her words.* A good man. A man who was likely just sick, although I later learned he'd recovered. I have no memory of him, left only with fragments of information my family has tried its best to share with me as I pieced together who my mother was as a young woman and mother.

My mother spent the next three years as a single mother, feeling vulnerable and alone, leaving her wide open for abusive predators to snatch her up, and us as well.

We moved from apartment to apartment, sometimes on our own, other times living with her next "knight in shining armor," who would always turn out to be a devil in disguise. The worst of whom came just before finally moving us to the safest of all havens, our maternal grandparents' home.

Memories are a funny thing. Sometimes they are crystal clear, while other times your mind can play tricks on you, causing you to believe that what you are recalling may be a dream, or rather a nightmare, or exaggerated. At least that is the way my mind worked. I had vague memories of my mother's boyfriends, one of them named Danny. My mother dated him when my sister and I were around four and five years old.

Danny lived on a beautiful property. I remember being there and spending a lot of time outside, *staying out of his way.* I don't recall exactly what my sister and I kept doing that caused his angry outbursts, but what I do recollect was an overall sense of always walking on eggshells around this man.

One memory played out in my mind pretty strongly, however. It was a hot and muggy afternoon in the summertime. My sister and I were playing outside. I cannot remember exactly what we were doing, but evidently it was something that, once again, pissed Danny off. He ordered Monica and me to go to his bedroom and get on the bed, and we listened. Moments later, he came in, ripped down both of our pants, and demanded that we bend over. He removed his belt and began to beat our naked backsides with it as we buried our cries into his disgusting sheets. I can remember peeking over at my sister, who was trying her best to be brave so that I would follow her cues. Whenever Danny hit us, Monica would give me the same familiar look, as if she could say by her face alone, *Just hold on, little sis; if you remain quiet, it will be over soon.*

I cannot remember if this was the final incident that ultimately prompted my mother to leave him, but eventually she did. From there, we went to live with our maternal grandparents on Wilson Drive in Syracuse. Years later, when I asked my family about Danny, they confirmed his abusive ways, though they hadn't realized what he had been doing to us until my mother thankfully had the strength to leave him. My mother always had to learn what was best for her the hard way, and in her own time.

Danny did try to come back for all of us, but my feisty grandmother saw to it he would never make that mistake again. One day he came to their home looking for my mother. He pushed his way through the door and into the house. My grandmother ordered him to leave and literally kicked him out the door and onto his pathetic, weak ass. She warned him never to come back, and if he did, she would call the police. He never returned.

When my mother was living back home, her family started to notice a change in her. They witnessed her becoming more anxious and riddled with worries about how she would handle everything.

Eventually, she sought help for her anxiety through medication alone. She received a prescription for valium. This "magic pill" seemed to give her all the things she was looking for, *and more of what she was not.*

My grandparents witnessed my mom become more and more dependent on the valium to alleviate her mental anguish. My family described a very scary time where my mother became distraught after one particular relationship broke up. To cope, she downed a few valiums and drinks, called her ex, and threatened to walk down Route 290 to end her life.

That was the first memory any family members had of my mother's suicidal ideations. No one categorized it for what it was—a mental illness—therefore she never received the proper treatment for it. It was a sign of the times; they didn't know any better then, nor did she. Certainly no one *ever* talked about it either, leaving my mother with no other choice, in her mind, but to suffer in silence, which she did, her entire life.

My mother went on to marry my stepfather on August 25, 1979, when I was six years old and just starting kindergarten. Their marriage lasted about ten years. A marriage full of his infidelity, cocaine addiction, physical abuse, and numerous nights of my mother trying to dull the pain with booze, sleeping pills, and marijuana. In truth, he was an awful man who used her. When they met, *she* was the one with a full-time job while raising two girls, while he lived off any handouts he could get. His father finally offered him a job at the company he worked for, allowing my mother the opportunity to be the stay-at-home and present mother she truly wanted to be for us. I believe she tried her best with the tools she had, which were scarce.

These were times of chaos with sprinkles of peace. When she and my stepfather finally decided to divorce, I was a selfish teenager wrapped up in my own life who couldn't see how terribly sad and alone my mother truly was.

Over the years, Mom's drinking worsened. I left for college, where I experienced my own fair share of partying, eventually leading to me flunking out for not showing up to class or doing any of the required assignments. I joined my mother in my grandmother's basement in Connecticut. There, we began to drink together, a dark and toxic bond.

Years later, I would meet my husband, Brian. During that time, I didn't fail to notice what was happening with my mom because I was too busy with my new life. No, *this* time was different. By then, I had built up a fair amount of anger and resentment over her behaviors and was sick of trying. The birth of my own children changed things, and I had to make a decision to take her as she was. When Brian and I became parents, during her sober times, my mother was a wonderful nana to my children.

When I look back at her life, my heart breaks over the chances she was never given or was too exhausted to take. She was not given the same opportunities I was, the fighting chance at life she fought for every day, until she decided she was no longer willing to.

Mom's life was hard, but we never talked about that. For the most part, if I ever asked her how she was, she never revealed her truth. Everything was "just fine" with her, when, in reality, she was suffering deeply with anxiety, depression, and addiction.

My beautiful, deeply flawed, loving mother tried for so many years to put a brave face on for the benefit of others. A price she paid for deeply on that warm May day.

A short time later, there I was, a mother myself, navigating through some of the same emotions I had watched my own mother struggle with. Emotions that plagued me, ones I would genetically stamp on my very own daughter.

I wanted to get back to being the woman I was before I lost my mom. The confident, unassuming, openhearted woman I always was. The anger that built, the resentment at her not being there, would kill me too *if I let it*. Connecting my heart to what my brain knew always ended the same way, as a misfire. I realized if I continued to torture myself over the reasons my mother's life ended, I would likely ruin my own.

But like mother, like daughter, I ultimately turned back to alcohol to help soothe my wounds.

My fortieth birthday was on November 16, 2013. Emotionally, I was still very much reeling, but turning forty prompted me to do many things, among them schedule some overdue doctor appointments; you know, all the usual "female stuff." I was a thyroid cancer survivor, almost twelve years out by then, and would have considered myself to be in good health. I completed the triathlon over the summer, just one month after my mother's death. Normally, my mom would have been the one I would have discussed those upcoming appointments with. She was always there for the important things.

The evening I received my thyroid cancer diagnosis, in the spring of 2002, I was alone in the kitchen when I picked up the phone and listened as the doctor apologized for calling so late and then proceeded to deliver the difficult news. The cells drawn in the biopsy were in fact cancerous, and he recommended having complete thyroidectomy surgery to remove the thyroid gland and any cancer.

For some time, I hadn't been feeling like myself. At first, I wrote it off, thinking perhaps I was just a worn-down new mom. I was always tremendously tired, and finally, when I couldn't seem to get rid of an eye infection I had contracted, that was the red flag necessary for me to finally make an appointment to see my primary care physician. She ordered some blood work and did a physical exam. During the exam, she checked my throat. She ran her fingertips around the outside of my neck. Up and down, my doctor carefully felt the front of my neck, paying special attention to the left side. I assumed she was feeling my glands without realizing she was particularly focused on my thyroid. My doctor said she felt a small lump, but reassured me that it was probably nothing. However, I should have an ultrasound just to be sure.

The ultrasound led my doctor to also order a biopsy. It was these results I received late that evening that caused my strong legs, which I could usually rely on to hold me up, to buckle beneath me. Slowly, I slithered to the floor as the doctor continued to explain what would happen next. But truthfully, I stopped comprehending anything she was saying after I heard the word "cancer."

I was only twenty-eight, my daughter barely over a year old.

I remember sitting on the cold kitchen tile floor. Brian was in our bedroom watching TV, and Bailey was sound asleep. She was still so little, so innocent. Brian and I were just starting our lives together as a married couple.

There I remained on that cold floor until I was able to gather enough physical and emotional strength to walk into the bedroom to tell Brian what that phone call was about.

I remember so many nights after that when I would lie in bed, crippled with anxiety. Dark thoughts of all the possible "what ifs." *What if they didn't get all the cancer? What if it spreads? Will it ever come back, and if it does, where will it go?* The doctor did warn me at the time that thyroid cancer can spread to the lymph nodes, then on to the lungs. That warning would remain in the back of my mind for some time, like some dark, ugly stain. I had enough knowledge about cancer, even back then, to know that if it spreads to your lungs, your chance of survival is not great.

But of all the worrisome thoughts that kept me up at night, the one that killed me the most was the thought of not being there for my daughter. *What if I don't get to see Bailey grow up? What if I die before she gets to really know her mom? This* was the most crippling thought of all. Unbearable thoughts would enter my mind when I let them creep through. Cancer brings on physical damage to the person who is fighting it, but the emotional damage it brings affects the entire family.

My mother understood my anxiety more than anyone else I knew, so I would turn to her to calm my overactive mind. Countless days she kept me company, keeping me busy and preoccupied so my thoughts wouldn't get the better of me. Many nights she came over to just sit with me so I didn't have to be alone with my thoughts. The worst part was the waiting, and my mom was there through it all.

I had my first of two thyroid surgeries in August 2002. I also underwent radioactive iodine treatments and other scans as a follow-up.

Brian and I were just beginning our lives together as a family when we faced this serious news. We met when we were in our early twenties; I was twenty-three and he was twenty-four. We worked together at a restaurant where he was a talented chef and I bartended, one of the many odd jobs I held back then.

Aside from my occasional pass through the kitchen if I needed something, or his when he came up to the bar for a cocktail after the kitchen closed, we didn't have many interactions. Besides, I was in a relationship. Although that one was pretty much ending, technically, I was spoken for. Brian was also seeing someone, not seriously, but we were both with other people, and neither one of us had enough nerve to strike up a real conversation.

Until one night, when Brian's shift had come to a close. I believe that particular night we served well over two hundred dinners and the bar was crankin'. Finally, when it slowed a little, most of the staff who were still there gathered at the bar with our regular customers, and Brian joined too. He stood toward the back of the crowd, shyly sipping his beer while his attention remained on me. *That* was the moment I knew there was something about this guy.

There he stood, so tall so as not to go unnoticed, though his height was not the reason he grabbed my attention that night.

It was simply the way he was looking at me. The bar was too crowded and much too loud for us to talk to each other, but every time our eyes met, he would cast his quirky and charming smile. The same smile that could light up a room and get everyone to respond, "Walleye!" (his nickname since high school).

The charmers I had met in the past had never really served me well. They were mostly musicians, not the productive type, more like the tortured artist type mixed in with the occasional real bad boy who never knew what it meant to be faithful. Young, foolish, and irresponsible, lustful love was most of my experience until Brian. He had a sincerity about him that earned the respect of everyone who met him.

We continued on from that night the way we always had, with the exception of finding more excuses to run into one another at work to exchange some flirtatious energy.

By now, the relationship I was in had ended, and I was talking about the breakup with one of the waitresses at the restaurant. Most of the crew knew Brian and I had a thing for each other, but I remained hesitant to hop into dating him, thinking the next relationship would just be a rebound one. My coworker listened to my concerns, then blurted out, "Ya know, you're about to lose the chance to date a really great guy here if you don't make a move soon. He thinks you're still on and off with that guy you were with. Move on from that loser! He cheated on you so my times. Brian would never treat you that way."

That conversation was the kick in the pants I needed to make a move. Summer was coming to an end and so was my seasonal bartending job. It appeared if Brian and I would ever get together outside of work, I would have to be the one to say something.

My last evening at work, at the end of the season, all I could think about was finding the right time to ask him out. Yup, *I* was going to ask *him* out on a date. I had *never* asked a man out on a date before! *What would I say, and what if he said no?* For my entire shift, my mind remained preoccupied by the thought of finding a way to ask Brian out.

Finally, my shift was coming to an end. Part of my closing responsibilities was to run downstairs for supplies to restock. On my way there, I ran into Brian in the stairwell, and I stopped him and started the conversation with, "Hey, tonight's my last night here, ya know."

He replied, "Yeah, it is…that sucks. You going to come back for the holiday season?"

"I'm not sure yet," I said. Then I just went for it. "We should go out some time."

He quickly responded, "Yes! That would be great! In fact, I have a family wedding to go to this weekend. Want to come?"

And so it began. I met his entire family on our very first date, all in one shot. He picked me up from my grandmother's house, where I was living at the time, and we headed off to his aunt's wedding.

It was certainly overwhelming to meet his big Italian family that evening. I remember walking across the dance floor, returning from the restroom to his grandfather shouting across the room, "Hey, Brian, where'd ya get this girl? New York City?" I wanted to crawl into a corner and hide from all the eyes that were now cast upon me. Brian's grandfather was just busting his chops, a characteristic that, over the years, I would come to love him for.

That night was the first of many dates in our love story. We worked hard and played even harder. Any downtime we had, we spent together, and it would usually involve doing something outdoorsy. Hiking, climbing, caving, and boating were just some of our activities, and they were almost always sure to include a few good beers and an even better wine.

Our first vacation was even more adventurous; it was also my first time on an airplane! We traveled to Aspen, Colorado, to visit one of his best high school buddies. We had an amazing time. We hiked thirteen thousand feet up Mount Sopris, went paragliding off a Colorado mountainside, and even skinny-dipped in the pool of a five-star resort! The trip proved to be incredibly memorable. So much so that on our last day there, Brian held our two plane tickets in his hands and swore he would rip them up right then and there if I agreed to stay.

We could easily have landed jobs at one of the local restaurants or hotels. Aspen was well supported by tourism, and his friend had lots of connections. There was a huge part of me that wanted to stay, but responsibility, and maybe fear of making such a spontaneous decision, ultimately held me back. I'd be lying if I said I look back with no regrets. Often, I wonder what it would have been like if we had ripped up our tickets and stayed.

Brian's courtship was romantic, thoughtful, and exciting. I knew he was getting close to asking me to marry him after about two years of dating. We began talking about buying a house, what type of house we would like to live in, and where. He had a plan that didn't come about overnight. He knew much earlier than I that he wanted to get married and start a family. He knew the day he asked me to marry him, as he already had the money to put down for a mortgage. I had no idea he had been putting that kind of money aside. When the time was right, the dreams and talks we had started to become more serious. So, we contacted a Realtor.

After a few short weeks of house hunting, he and his father came across an adorable beach home in a cozy lake community. It was small at just under twelve hundred square feet, but it was just right for a starter house. Brian was so excited to show it to me. I went back with him the very next day to have a look. As soon as I walked into the kitchen, I fell in love. I believe the kitchen was half the house! The previous owners had just added it on. It was perfect for us, especially for Brian as a chef. He put in an offer, and a few short days later it was accepted.

We moved in on New Year's Eve. A new year and a new home. We spent that New Year's Eve unpacking boxes and sipping champagne. Suddenly, we heard fireworks booming over the mountain range in our backyard. The view was magical, just like the start of our lives together. That evening, we made love on the bare floor of our unfurnished living room.

Seven months after moving in, Brian proposed. It was Fourth of July weekend 1997, and my sister and nephew had come for a visit. It was the first time they were going to see our new home. These were exciting times, full of promise.

Brian told me he was going out the first night my sis was going to be here because a bunch of his friends were coming in from out of town for the holiday weekend, including the friend we had visited in Colorado. While I didn't really mind that he was going out, I asked that he *please* not get too banged up or be late and embarrass me in front of my sister. Well, needless to say, he did both of the things I had begged him not to and also came home with a *huge* black eye from wrestling around, like an idiot, with a friend. Brian took a head butt right to the eye. When he arrived home like that, I was pissed! I refused to sleep in the same bed with him and wouldn't argue with his foolish drunken ass. I chose to sleep on the tiny couch in our office, desperately trying to keep my sister and nephew, who were sleeping a short distance away in our living room, from hearing us fight.

The next morning, Brian pulled his hungover ass out of bed and started kissing me. "I planned a really great day for us," he said sweetly. "You, me, and a bunch of our friends are going to go skydiving!" Now, skydiving is something I had always wanted to try, and my sister would be leaving that day anyway. Nothing about the previous evening was addressed, as my excitement and nervousness about the day ahead replaced any anger I still had been feeling toward him.

When we arrived at Blue Sky Skydiving Ranch, we were joined by about a dozen of our closest friends. After filling out the necessary forms to waive the company of any liability in case we accidently died, the jumpmasters led us to a Volkswagen bus, where we watched a ten-minute instructional video on skydiving 101. That was it, a brief bit of instruction, and off we went.

We were each assigned to a jumpmaster and methodically loaded into the plane, where I was seated in the back. I remember being a bit frustrated that my jumpmaster told me to go to the back of the plane, because I assumed that meant I would be one of the last ones to jump...my assumption was right.

One by one, I watched as my friends jumped out of a perfectly good airplane that was flying at around fifteen thousand feet.

Then, it was my turn. Marc, my jumpmaster, slid me all the way to the edge of the door. No matter how I try to describe it, nothing can convey how loud it is to be in an airplane with the door open.

This was it, time to plummet toward the earth! There were only a few seconds between the time it took me to slide toward the door and when I leaped from the airplane. No time to think, just do.

I fell fast and furiously at about 140 mph, although it didn't seem like it. The sensation of freefalling was not like I'd expected. In fact, it wasn't anything like I anticipated. There was no awareness of the speed at which I was plummeting toward the earth. When my parachute opened, my wild ride became ever so peaceful. I was like a feather floating through the air. Everything became quieter, allowing for me and my jumpmaster to talk with each other.

He pointed to the beautiful scenery, showing me gorgeous farms, local ponds, and nearby ledges people liked to go rock climbing on. The ledges were magnificent, but I was glad they were far enough away that we didn't have to maneuver around them!

My instructor steered our chute around and around and then asked me, "Do you think this is a good place to land?"

What? Shouldn't he know where to land? Why the hell was he asking me?

I replied, "I have no idea!"

He directed me to look down to my right, where I could vaguely make out a large blue tarp surrounded by a bunch of people I assumed were my friends.

The closer we got, the more easily I could make out what was painted on the tarp: "Will you marry me?" I asked my instructor what was going on, and he said, "That's for you, kid!"

Brian was proposing to me! Holy crap, it was really happening. We landed semisoftly on our backsides. My jumpmaster released me from the tandem hold to the sweetest moments that awaited me next…

The moment he proposed to me. He knelt down on one knee and asked, "Will you marry me, Valerie?"

I quickly replied, "Yes," and hugged and kissed him so quickly he didn't even have the chance to put the ring on my finger! When he finally did, I looked around at all our friends, who were cheering and crying happy tears for us. Then I noticed my sister, who I thought had already headed back home to Syracuse, there, holding my nephew. Alongside my sister, stood my mother and my soon-to-be in-laws.

Brian had organized almost everyone we cared about to be there to share in that special moment. It was amazing; just like his entire courtship, always making me feel special and loved.

By 2013, Brian and I had been married for fourteen years and were the parents of two beautiful children. I needed to do my due diligence to remain in good physical health, for my family. Having a mammogram was just another check mark on the list of appointments I made for myself before the end of the shittiest year of my life.

Blessed with itty-bitty, little titties made up of very dense breast tissue meant that, along with a mammogram, I also needed an ultrasound. Both were done at our local Woman's Imaging Center.

When I walked into my appointment, the first thing I noticed was how much the center had changed in just the three years since I had been there. The hospital had transformed it so it no longer gave off the sterile, cold feeling most waiting rooms did. This one was decorated in the pink color scheme that had become the popular one for breast cancer awareness. Victorian-style decor adorned the little, cozy space where I waited for my name to be called. I sat, checking my phone and leafing through outdated magazines.

It was only a short time before my name was called. The technician led me to a tiny changing room and asked me to please undress from the waist up and put on one of those most "fashionable" hospital gowns. She waited for me in the next room, where I would be having my mammogram. During the test, both my left and right breasts were squeezed at what I can only assume is every "normal" angle needed to take the necessary images. When she finished, I waited in another room to give the radiologist an opportunity to look at the images before I headed in to get the ultrasound.

Throughout my life, I have had more ultrasounds than I can count. The first one was when I found out I was pregnant with Bailey. Of course, it's normal to have many ultrasounds during pregnancy. *They* are the ones you look forward to, a chance to see your baby and how it is developing. You get to hear its heartbeat and, if you want, you can also find out if you are having a boy or a girl. We didn't find out with Bailey. Brian and I had decided to keep that a surprise. Then there was my experience with having the biopsy that led to my thyroid cancer diagnosis. It was no wonder I was having reservations about any type of testing. I reassured myself that my nervous reaction was normal and longed for my mother's presence to do the same.

Ugh, I was almost forty. I wondered if it would be like this from now on—an endless number of preemptive strikes against all the "what-ifs" that could happen to my body as the years crept by. "Fuck that" is what I wanted to say, but instead, I thanked the nurses and technicians for their time and went home to wait for someone to call with my results.

Three days passed before one of the nurses from the Women's Imaging Center called to tell me they'd spotted suspicious calcifications that were new since the last mammogram, done three years before. She told me they wanted to do a magnified view, with another mammogram of the left breast only, and asked if I would come in the following day.

The next day, alone, I went back to the Women's Imaging Center, where they repeated the same protocol as before, only this time they only took pictures of my left breast. They torqued my breast in so many different angles, a very painful appointment, but I did not dare complain because I wanted to be sure they got what they were after. I was certain not to rush something that serious. Plus, the thought of going back to do it all over again was enough motivation to tolerate having my breast manipulated like Play-Doh.

After they were finished the technician asked me to wait while she showed the magnified images to the radiologist. When she returned, she informed me they were able to get all the pictures they needed, and someone would be calling me in a few days with the results.

This time, when I received that concerning phone call and wanted to call my mother to calm my fears, I couldn't. It had been only five months since laying her to rest. I felt alone, motherless, rudderless.

Two days later, the same technician called to tell me they planned to order a stereotactic core biopsy of the left breast because the calcifications on the magnified image appeared irregular in their shape. She proceeded to give me almost the same speech every health care professional had given me when I awaited my thyroid biopsy results: "Don't worry. Almost all biopsies come back benign." I understood she was just trying to calm my fears, a job usually left for my mother. The nurse had no way of knowing about my vast experience with that scripted line of bullshit.

As I awaited the results, my fortieth birthday came and went without much thought other than how to prepare for my biopsy at the end of that long-drawn-out November. I tried to stay busy with work and did spend my actual birthday on a fun, surprise, celebratory hike with close friends and family. At that time no one except my husband knew about my recent health scare. I hadn't wanted to concern anyone unnecessarily. They had all ridden this rodeo circus with me before, and I felt guilty selling admission tickets to it again. For the moment, there was no need to worry anyone about the biopsy or anything else until I had more information.

I don't remember feeling very nervous when the morning of my core needle biopsy arrived. The one I had on my thyroid was fairly painless. Of course, having my mother's hand to hold during that experience likely helped tremendously. Now, I was left to try to draw from my own inner strength. Left to scrape up remnants of life lessons, lessons I'd forgotten to take notes on. My mother was only fifty-nine when she swallowed a fistful of antidepressants and sleeping pills. God damn it, *she should be here with me.*

I wanted to hold her hand and couldn't. All the feelings surrounding her suicide were not even things I was allowed to talk about, because my sister and I had decided together, from the very beginning, not to tell anyone how our mother *really* died, mostly to protect our grandmother, her mom. It hurts enough to lose someone so suddenly, but to lose someone to suicide—that's a whole different storm to maneuver through, a shitstorm of emotions that would prove to be immensely stressful and confusing as the months and years went on. As I navigated through my heartache, close friends tried to reassure me that it was "normal" to continue to grieve in whatever amount of time I needed to. But what the fuck is "normal" grief when your mother kills herself, especially right before a time I so desperately needed her?

I feel angry when I remember she wasn't there when I needed her. No one could replace what she could have done for me in that moment.

My mother's hand was replaced by my husband's. Brian always tried the best he could. He held my hand for as long as possible, but they would not let him in the room with me; it was going to be a mammogram-guided needle biopsy and "the radiation is not something he should electively be exposed to." Those kinds of statements made me a bit nervous...*the radiation was not good for others but okay for me?* I felt, at this point, as if my boobs were apt to glow like two headlamps from all the images that had been taken of them in those last few weeks!

They did allow Brian to stay while they explained the procedure to both of us. In this kind of biopsy, a large, hollow needle is used to draw the sample. First, they numb the breast with anesthesia. Next, the radiologist uses the needle to remove several cylinder-shaped samples of tissue from the suspicious area. When the radiologist gets the necessary sample, they extract it and place a small metal clip on the breast to mark the site, in case the tissue samples are cancerous and more surgery is required. Sounds simple, right? After everything was explained, they asked if I had any questions. I didn't, so they excused Brian and led me to the room where my biopsy would be performed.

The entire procedure was done while I sat upright in a chair that could be reclined if necessary. To start, there were two technicians there with me. I asked them if we could pray together before they started. They both politely obliged. Together, we held hands while I spoke a simple prayer for God to be with the technicians, the radiologist, and me during the testing. In saying the words out loud to God, I gave whatever the results may be, and the procedure itself, to Him. I have always shared with my elementary school-aged Confraternity of Christian Doctrine students that when you talk with God, that *is* praying, and it is okay to pray specifically for what you need. In that moment, I specifically needed to give all my worries to God. In truth, they felt like hollow words.

Before the technicians sat me down in the chair where I would remain throughout the entire procedure, I reached in to my pocket for a worry stone that I kept with me during times when I felt like I needed to be close to my mom, which was pretty much always. It was a small, clear stone with an angel in the center. I'd found it in my mother's house after she passed, while we were cleaning it out.

Soon after my mom died, I traveled to Syracuse to help make arrangements with my sister. After Monica left for the day, I was alone in my mother's home. Still in shock at her passing, I stood at the kitchen sink, washing vases we would leave behind for the auctioneer. I wept out loud, all alone. Well, not really alone—her two cats, Ziggy and Iggy, were there to keep me company. However, these usually very vocal Siamese were oddly quiet the entire time I was there. Maybe they were experiencing the same feelings I was: utter shock and anguishing pain. As I stood at the sink, I began talking out loud to my mom as if she were sitting in the next room and could hear me. It was the first weekend of June; the air was warm and there was a gentle breeze that would come every now and again. I welcomed that breeze, because when it came, the wind chimes in her garden would start to sing. That sound always reminded me of her. The first gift she gave Brian and me when we moved into our home was a set of wind chimes.

There I stood, begging for some sign from my mother to reassure me that she was okay. Moments later, I noticed this beautiful stone sitting inside a candle on top of the windowsill above the sink. I picked it up and decided that was a good enough sign for the moment. Little did I know that for years after her death, I would continue to search for signs that she was at peace.

I took the stone out of my pocket moments before the biopsy on my breast began.

The procedure took a little over an hour. I wouldn't say it was painful, but it was definitely very uncomfortable. When it was finished I walked over to a different room where I waited to speak with the radiologist. But before I could, a technician entered the room looking very disappointed. "I am so sorry, Valerie," she said, "but we didn't get any of the calcifications on that try. We are going to have to repeat the entire procedure if you are up for it."

You have got to be kidding me! I thought. I was able to get through the last biopsy okay; I really didn't know if I had it in me to do another one. But what choice did I have? There was no way in hell they were going to get me back there another day. I recognized the facts—that if I didn't do what was necessary to make sure there was nothing wrong with me, I likely would never have returned.

"Okay, let's do this," I answered, and after a short break to recover, it was back to the proverbial square one.

I sent Brian off to get things taken care of with the kids. There wasn't much he could do from the waiting room, and I needed him to get Collin off the bus and go to Bailey's parent/teacher conference.

Brian had changed professions soon after our daughter was born. Witnessing the stress the food service industry—especially being a chef—induces in individuals and their families made him rethink what he wanted to do professionally. He'd begun working for a friend of his, doing siding and roofing and, within two short years, decided to go out on his own. He became a builder, opening Source Construction Services. It was a brave move that paid off in more time for his family and friends.

The second time around, the procedure took about the same length of time, but I believe my body had reached its breaking point. I remember hearing the radiologist say they were almost done and just about to put in the clip. At that point, I really was not feeling well. On my way to passing out, I told the technician I was going down, and the last thing I remember was seeing her open a tube of ammonia for me to sniff to stay alert. But it was too late. I'm not sure how long I was out, but when I woke up, I had no idea where I was or what had happened. Disorientated, I looked around and noticed a few nurses from the ER and a physician's assistant I recognized for two reasons: Recently he had put stitches—eight, to be exact—in my son's chin after Collin fell in our kitchen and split his chin open *and* he used to take my spinning classes. Great, there I was, his spinning instructor, tits out and totally embarrassed. Small town living at its finest, where everyone knows your name, and apparently…your tits too.

So, there I lay, gown open, left breast bleeding, and totally exhausted. The radiologist and the two technicians who were with me on that very long testing episode took tremendous care of me. Not only did they display compassion, they also communicated with me frequently, keeping me at ease. After my blood pressure stabilized, I was wheeled into an adjacent room to recover and get the bleeding to stop so one final image could be taken to see if they'd gotten the sample they needed. The problem was, I didn't stop bleeding.

An hour passed until I was finally able to convince them that maybe if they just Steri-stripped the area, they could get a quick, light compression image and I might finally be able to leave. I had been there since eight in the morning and it was already going on four o'clock in the afternoon. All in agreement, they brought me back to the mammogram machine to take that one last picture. The results. . . drumroll, please. . . the radiologist was able to get all he needed, and I was free to go home with the promise that if the bleeding continued, I would have my husband bring me to the ER.

I can sum up my experience with the core needle biopsy by saying it was like going to the gynecologist for a Pap smear and walking out with a baby!

As soon as I arrived home, I went straight to bed. All I had eaten that day were crackers, cookies, and juice, so Brian fixed me something to eat and delivered it to our room. When I sat up to make myself comfortable, a sharp pain shot within my left breast. *Crap, that can't be good*, I thought to myself. I removed my clothes to discover I was bleeding right through the dressings. Out of pure exhaustion, I started to whimper. I'd been at the hospital all day;

that was the last place I wanted to return, but it appeared as if I had no choice—the bleeding was too much.

Luckily, I did not end up having to wait long in the ER at all; we got right in. The doctor glued both incision sites right up and, once again, I was good to go. We had dropped the kids off at our neighbor's house on the way and decided to leave them there overnight so I could rest. That evening, I fell fast asleep, praying I would not waken to déjà vu.

THREE

Knowledge Is Power

"All the resources we need are in the mind."

~THEODORE ROOSEVELT

THE RADIOLOGIST HAD WARNED ME I WOULD HAVE TO make it through the weekend before getting my results and it would likely be my gynecologist who would call me. Doing what most people do to keep from thinking about what lays heaviest on their mind, I stayed busy. Only this time, without my mom around to keep me company. Still recovering from the procedure, I decided to start decorating for Christmas to keep myself occupied. Christmas was one month away, and my family loved the holiday season. Starting to decorate in November wasn't unusual for us.

Monday came and went without news, which I took as a good sign. Tuesday arrived and I needed to head into work, then I had lunch plans at my girlfriend's home later.

Shortly after arriving at my friend's home, Brian called my cell. He told me that my gynecologist had just phoned our house looking for me, and he told him to try my cell. I forewarned my friend and the other girls who were there that I may have to excuse myself during lunch to take a call. Up until then, no one other than immediate family knew what was going on. They, of course, understood. Sure enough, just as we sat down to eat, my phone rang again. I excused myself from the table and went into the next room to talk to my doctor.

He informed me that some abnormal cells were, in fact, found in the biopsy and I needed to see him that day to discuss the results. I silently returned to the table and tried my best to rejoin the conversation, but my friends could see that something was wrong. According to my face, I was doing a horrible job of pretending everything was okay. It was one of those moments when you are there but not *really* there. The ladies reassured me that they would understand if I wanted to leave right away, but I didn't want to be rude. My friend had prepared a beautiful lunch for us—homemade salmon cakes over a colorful green salad. I continued to sit quietly with the ladies, eating my food without tasting it, moving the greens around the plate like my son did when he didn't feel like eating.

I tried to listen, but was unable to engage in conversation. I wasn't able to get where I needed to go off my mind, and they could see that. "Valerie, go. We totally understand," one of my girlfriends sweetly said. With that, I ate and ran…well, technically, drove, to my doctor's office.

When I arrived at my gynecologist's office, I was taken to his office instead of the examining room where I was used to seeing him. He handed me a copy of the written surgical pathology report from my biopsy. The diagnosis was highlighted.

"Lobular Carcinoma in Situ, negative for invasive carcinoma." *What did that mean?* To better understand it, my doctor referred me to a breast surgeon in Danbury, Connecticut. I went home and immediately called for an appointment. Luckily, they were able to fit me in right away; I would only have to wait three days. Handling the feeling of not knowing what was medically going on with me was something I had done before, so three days wasn't so bad. When I had to wait to find out more about my thyroid cancer, I hadn't had the convenience of Dr. Google. Things were a lot different now than they had been almost twelve years before. This time around I had the power to find out anything I wanted to learn right at my fingertips. So, I typed four simple letters into the search bar to learn more about them:

LCIS: (BreastCancer.org) LCIS – Lobular Carcinoma In Situ

Lobular carcinoma in situ (LCIS) is an area (or areas) of abnormal cell growth that increases a person's risk of developing invasive breast cancer later on in life. Lobular means that the abnormal cells start growing in the lobules, the milk-producing glands at the end of breast ducts. Carcinoma refers to any cancer that begins in the skin or other tissues that cover internal organs — such as breast tissue. In situ or "in its original place" means that the abnormal growth remains inside the lobule and does not spread to surrounding tissues. People diagnosed with LCIS tend to have more than one lobule affected.

Despite the fact that its name includes the term "carcinoma," LCIS is not a true breast cancer. Rather, LCIS is an indication that a person is at higher-than-average risk for getting breast cancer at some point in the future. For this reason, some experts prefer the term "lobular neoplasia" instead of "lobular carcinoma." A neoplasia is a collection of abnormal cells.

LCIS is usually diagnosed before menopause, most often between the ages of 40 and 50. Less than 10 percent of women diagnosed with LCIS have already gone through menopause. LCIS is extremely uncommon in men.

LCIS is viewed as an uncommon condition, but we don't know exactly how many people are affected. That's because LCIS does not cause symptoms and usually does not show up on a mammogram. It tends to be diagnosed as a result of a biopsy performed on the breast for some other reason.

My brain fixates on the sentence in the second paragraph: "LCIS is not a true breast cancer. Rather LCIS is an indication that a person is at higher-than-average risk for getting breast cancer at some point in the future."

Did that mean I didn't have breast cancer? I tried my best not to jump to conclusions. My goal was to gather enough information to line up some questions for the doctor on Friday, at the same time being cautious not to overwhelm myself, trying especially hard not to read anything that didn't pertain to me. I concluded I'd had enough of playing Dr. Google and logged off my computer to wait for my real doctor to review my results with me.

Friday's appointment couldn't get there soon enough. Brian came with me, which was very helpful. This way, if I missed any important information, there was a second set of listening ears. I booked two appointments for that day: one with the first doctor recommended by my gynecologist and another to get a second opinion. The doctor and nurse entered the examining room. She examined both breasts before going over my diagnosis and treatment options. The doctor noticed the trauma of the ordeal I'd gone through just a week earlier from the biopsy; bruising on the left breast was still very visible, and she remarked that it must not have gone smoothly. Her nurse measured the length and width of both my arms. This was something new. I asked her why she had to take those measurements. She explained, "In case of any swelling, we need to take a baseline measurement." I assumed she was referring to lymphedema. In my field as a personal trainer and exercise instructor, I had worked with many cancer survivors who suffered from lymphedema and was pretty familiar with it.

After the exam the doctor sat down to thoroughly explain what LCIS was. The first thing she said to me was that I did not have breast cancer. She confirmed what I had read, that the medical community did not think of LCIS as breast cancer anymore, but rather as precancerous cells the appearance of which increased my risks of having a more invasive type of breast cancer. It was labeled as breast cancer years ago, and now it was kind of like having to rename a child; the first name sticks, so sometimes people were still told they had breast cancer.

She continued to explain that the next step would be a lumpectomy to rule out that this may be something more and, after the lumpectomy, we would discuss treatment options. It was crystal clear to me that she wasn't going to discuss what those might look like at this time, but she did reassure me that I would not have to have any chemotherapy. That was a *huge* weight off my mind, because that was going to be the deciding factor for what and when Brian and I would tell our kids anything. Up until that point, they weren't aware of anything that was going on with me medically.

My children knew I was a survivor of thyroid cancer. For many years our family participated in numerous fundraisers to raise awareness for all cancers and raise money for research. At some of those events, I was represented as a cancer survivor. But I wasn't ready to discuss this new diagnosis with them until I had all my information and a plan in place first. Before my appointment with the breast surgeon, Brian and I discussed the possibility that if I had to undergo chemotherapy, there would obviously be no way to hide anything from the kids. We would have to sit them down to have a much harder conversation. That would be a game changer for our family. Hearing no chemo was an immediate relief.

That first appointment prompted more questions. Thankfully, I had a little time in the car to gather my thoughts as we headed to the next doctor's office. The protocol was much the same; she conducted her examination and offered another explanation of my diagnosis. She was aware I had just come from seeing another surgeon and asked what my questions were for her, but this doctor seemed to be a little more open to having a conversation about possible treatment options. Our question-and-answer session went something like this:

Me: "Let me get this straight: If I get the lumpectomy, you are doing it to see if all that's there is LCIS and nothing more, right?"

Doctor: "Yes, that is correct."

Me: "If that is the case, then I would have to go on a preventive treatment plan. What would that be?"

Doctor: "You would likely have two mammograms per year with an ultrasound as well. We would also highly recommend you take a drug such as Tamoxifen as a preventive treatment. Tamoxifen is a hormone [antiestrogen] therapy for hormone receptor–positive breast cancer patients in premenopausal woman mostly."

From what I was able to understand, some breast cancer cells required estrogen to grow. Estrogen binds to and activates these cells. Tamoxifen can block the growth of these cells. However, it also could come with a boatload of side effects, so my next question, of course, was, "What are the side effects of Tamoxifen?"

What followed sounded like a commercial for any drug company!

When taking Tamoxifen, there are risks of other types of cancer developing, such as endometrial cancer, uterine cancer. It may also cause some cardiovascular and metabolic problems. It may cause a rapid increase in triglycerides, increase the risk of thromboembolism [blood clot], and may cause fatty liver. Tamoxifen may also affect your central nervous system. Some studies have shown evidence of reduced cognition. Also, a significant number of patients have experienced reduction of libido.

Well, that's where she lost Brian…right at lack of libido! I asked the doctor if there were any other treatment options.

She replied, "Yes…having a bilateral mastectomy."

Now, I knew a little bit about what a bilateral mastectomy was. Unfortunately, a few of my girlfriends had been through worse, having breast cancer and the bilateral mastectomy, with reconstruction done. Thankfully, those women remained healthy. When the doctor reviewed this option with me, I immediately knew what I was going to choose. For me, it was clear. I recognized the map to this road if I chose to travel it. A road full of waiting, "scanxiety," and monitoring. I did *not* want to be a slave to the technology that was going to determine whether my cells had disappeared forever or decided to come back with a fury. My mental health was worth more to me than my breasts.

Anxiety was a familiar enemy. Having been through this once before with my thyroid cancer, I was *not* willing to revisit that torment. Also, the thought of taking a medicine that may or may not wreak havoc on me wasn't appealing.

I took only a few moments to let the information swirl around in my brain before I broke it down to two choices.

First option: have a lumpectomy to get all the LCIS and rule out anything else. A preventive treatment plan would be put in place that would include scans, and who knew if they would see everything in the mammogram and ultrasound, not to mention expose me to more radiation. I would also be taking the dreaded Tamoxifen for at least five years.

Second option: the bilateral mastectomy with reconstruction and no preventive treatment plan to speak of, as the issue would be literally gone, the issue being…my breasts.

I continued to think to myself before I revealed to the doctor my concerns of anxiety and my experience with battling the anxiety itself more than the actual thyroid cancer. I began to reflect back on all those sleepless nights and likely the same "what-ifs," that would plague me. Only this time I would wake in the morning with no mother to call. No mother to carry me through any of this. My heart sank and I began to cry. The doctor handed me a tissue. I regained my composure so I could ask her what choice she would make if she were me. Pausing only for a moment, she grabbed both my hands and answered, "Bilateral mastectomy with reconstruction."

Knowledge is power; now it was up to me.

FOUR

Reality Bites

"Face reality as it is, not as it was or as you wish it to be."

~JACK WELCH

SPEAKING WITH A LOVED ONE ABOUT HAVING A BILATERAL mastectomy is not easy, and when it came to doing so with my husband, it felt like a horrendous task. I'm not sure I even gave much thought to how *he* would take it. Brian was a strong, hardworking, loyal, and supportive man. He was also a vault, a man of few words, but with a heart full of emotion. I knew that my decision to have the bilateral mastectomy may have come quickly to me, but I imagined that the transition for both of us would be unknown and take some time.

Would he like my new body? More important, would *I* like my new body, maybe even eventually learn to love myself again? I was feeling so out of touch with my emotions. I went from grieving my mother to making a decision to save my life. It was a staggering time. That is how I felt most days, staggering by, trying to get through it all. Consuming me were thoughts of going through all this without my mother. I'd just lost her; now would I lose my breasts too? It was too much. I had to lean on my husband, and this was not something I found easy to do. Knowing my mother was abandoned by my birth father and then my stepfather had provided very poor examples of what marriage was all about. Even though my marriage to Brain was very different from what I'd witnessed throughout my childhood, there was still a bit of caution there. Hesitation about how much I could actually rely on another person, especially my husband, was always something I struggled with. After all, aside from my uncle Bill and my grandfather, both of whom were now with my mother, the only men in my life proved to be pieces of shit. Until I met Brian.

"Brian, they will take my nipples when I have the surgery," I reluctantly explained to him. I loved my nipples and he did too. Would Brian miss them as much as I would? I continued, "From what I understand, I will lose sensation in both my breasts." I knew they would look and feel different to me, and I couldn't help wondering, as I reviewed all this with Brian, how he would react when all was said and done. How would this affect our sex life, our marriage?

We both sat on the end of our bed. He said nothing as I cried. I didn't need him to say anything; just being with him at that moment made me feel safe.

When he finally decided to speak, he simply reassured me. "I love you, always. Besides, you have a sweet ass!" Oddly enough, at that moment it was the comic relief we both needed.

Now, I also needed to try my best to trust his love for me. I owed it to us not to let the stamp of abandonment still embedded deep within my being affect our marriage.

However, I began to wonder about the grief my husband would face. No one really ever talks about that. How could I not think about him when I knew my pain *was* his pain? Real love between two people—when you love someone body and soul—sexual love, physical love, and spiritual love, was all intertwined. Would my decision to alter the physical and sexual part of our love damage us forever? I wanted to believe that our commitment to our marriage, our children, and each other would be enough to overcome something like this.

Anyone going through a health scare will tell you that sometimes the worst part is the waiting and not moving forward with an answer or a plan. At this point, I had my answer: a diagnosis. I had my plan, although it wasn't being put into action yet. Now I needed to firm things up by finding the breast surgeon to perform the bilateral mastectomy, along with a plastic surgeon to do the reconstruction. They would work together as a team. Finding the perfect match was very important because they would do the surgery together. First, the breast surgeon would remove my breasts, and then the plastic surgeon would take over and insert the expanders for the reconstructive part and close me up. My need to simplify the description of the surgery was one of survival. One thing that was on my side was time. Time to make the right choices for me, including when to have the surgery and who would perform it.

In the coming weeks, Brian and I continued to speak at length about my decision. Even saying that always sounded selfish to me: "my decision," not "our decision." Like when expectant parents say, "We're pregnant" rather than "She's pregnant." I am sorry, fellas, but until you can, in fact, carry a child, *she* is pregnant, not both of you! This was my body, my decision, and Brian never once questioned it. From the beginning, he was always very reassuring that he was on board with whatever decisions I made for myself concerning my health. He didn't really know anything about bilateral mastectomies or reconstruction, but he trusted me enough to do what was right for me. I thought about looking online for more information to help us, but I was not ready to play Dr. Google once again searching for images of what "it" may look like, and I was horrified at the thought of showing any to Brian. I would look when I was ready. Besides, I wanted to find the right ones to share with him that would help us both to cope. We needed to prepare as best we could.

We went on to discuss the logistics of how I would face a bunch of upcoming doctor appointments. With him being a self-employed contractor, I wanted to make sure I only asked him to take time off when I really needed him to. I knew he was stressed. Being a business owner comes with an enormous amount of worry. He played it off well, but I knew some days his head must have felt like it was about to explode. He carried his business with him all the time, day and night. Constantly concerned with making sure he had enough work lined up to keep his guys busy and enough capital in the bank to back his business up during the slow periods. He tried his best to manage his time between family and work, as well as supervising his employees. When you own a small business, a fair amount of uncertainty goes with it. I hated the fact that I was adding to his long list of things to think about. But that was life; there were no guarantees, and we had to find ways to manage all my upcoming appointments and the help I would need while recovering.

Truthfully, I did not need him there for every single appointment. Together, we planned how to handle the kids' schedules while I recovered and wouldn't be able to drive, who would cook, who would clean, who would make sure everything that I usually did would be taken care of, all the little details that go along with recovering from major surgery. I was the worrier in the family. Brian's response to almost everything I stressed about was always the same: "Don't worry, it will all work out." With my type A personality, I always had a hard time letting go. Which was why getting things lined up and a surgery date settled was something I looked forward to. Being organized helped provide relief to me in very stressful situations—or rather, in this case, chapters in my life!

The next few days were business as usual. Brian and I occasionally talked about my mastectomy, but as life tends to do, it went on. That is, until something happens to remind you of what you are trying to forget thinking about.

Up early and getting ready for work, I found myself standing naked in front of the mirror across from our bathroom, about to put on my sports bra. Brian was in the bathroom next to me, also getting ready for the day. Playfully, I placed both of my hands under my breasts to prop them up, making them appear larger and perkier. I turned to Brian to show him and said in jest, "Think I should get boobs like this?" To which he replied, "Is that why you are doing this, for the big tits?"

I screamed at him, although he didn't deserve it; he was just responding to my joking around. That *is* what I loved about him—his sense of humor—but in this case his timing was not impeccable. His words penetrated me. I lost my temper and continued to lay in to him: "How could you even think that? Do you have any idea what it looks like when you have reconstruction? It's not a boob job! Don't expect them to look like nice fake tits cuz they won't! You have no fucking idea what this is going to look like!"

He didn't have any idea, and how could I have expected him to? Now he felt awful, and so did I. I asked him to get out of the bathroom so I could use it. "Wait," he said, "I was kidding! I was totally joking!" I couldn't even let him know that I knew he wasn't being serious. There was a huge lump in my throat that prevented me from doing so.

"Please, just get out for a second, *please*," I begged him, and he conceded. I shut and locked the door, allowing myself to continue to sob some more, running water in the shower in a feeble attempt to muffle my sounds so the kids wouldn't hear them. This time, as I stared into the bathroom mirror, all of the humor was gone. I was scared. I peered at my face, then looked down at my breasts—now covered in shame by my sports bra—and back up at my face again. "You can do this, Valerie," I told myself. "They are only tits."

I felt horrible for making Brian feel bad. I knew he hadn't said what he had because he felt that way. He'd said it in response to my lightheartedness about the subject so far, and I knew better. The truth was, I knew he would love me if I decided to cut off my breasts and left them off, if I didn't go through with the painful reconstruction. The question still remained: Would I love myself and my new body that way? Would *I* accept the choice I was about to make?

Time would tell. What I did know for sure was that my worry about having a healthy body outweighed my concerns for my own body image. I realized the emotional impact would likely be significant, but I also knew that my spirit, on most days, was still strong. I would be damned if I would allow what society or what biologically defined me as a woman to be what I based my decision on. I knew what really defined being a woman meant to me, and that…was my spirit. However, the world seemed to be trying to attack it lately, and I was starting to question just how much more I could take.

I splashed some cold water on my face and opened the door to find Brian standing just outside. "I'm sorry," I told him. "I am just all over the place." He pulled me in for a hug and didn't speak; his embrace said it all.

FIVE

My Lovely Lady Lumps

"Chin up, tits off, onward."

~VALERIE WALSH

AFTER SEEKING A FEW MORE PROFESSIONAL OPINIONS, I continued my research to find the right breast surgeon. I went back to the first doctor I saw in Danbury. She had more experience performing this type of surgery and her résumé was very impressive. At our first consultation, we had tentatively set up an appointment for me to have my lumpectomy in early December 2013. Before we could proceed with the surgery, I would need a clip placed back on my left breast to mark the biopsy. In most cases when you have a biopsy, as mentioned earlier, they leave a little metal clip in your breast to mark the area, so if a lumpectomy is required, the surgeon will know where to operate. However, the clip was removed accidentally when I passed out during that long-drawn-out day at the Women's Imaging Center. Now, I needed to have it replaced.

Even though the appointment for the lumpectomy was already scheduled, I hesitated. I was confused about why I needed to go through these two procedures—the wire biopsy and the lumpectomy—when I knew I would ultimately go with the bilateral mastectomy with reconstruction. During my next visit with the surgeon, I brought up my concerns.

"Doctor, please tell me why I still need to do this. I've already made my decision, so it seems unnecessary," I began.

The surgeon explained, "The lumpectomy is to rule out having to take any lymph nodes when you do have your mastectomy, Valerie. We try to avoid having to remove any sentinel lymph nodes unless the results of the lumpectomy indicate there is something more." She continued, "Then if more is found, we will deal with it during the mastectomy. We are trying to avoid that because it becomes an even more painful surgery to recover from."

Her voice was more sterile than her office. It matched her personality. One would have thought I would choose the doctor who held my hands and told me that she would make the choice to have a mastectomy if she were in my shoes. But I didn't. I wanted the doctor who came with more credentials, and this one was it.

Although I was really dreading the clip placement and wire biopsy because of my last experience, what she told me made sense. Ultimately, by this point I had made the decision that she would be my breast surgeon, so it was time to start trusting her advice.

The clip placement procedure was done two days before my lumpectomy with no issues.

When the day for my lumpectomy came, I arranged for the kids to go to my mother-in-law's house after school in case things took longer than expected.

They were running on time at the hospital and got me right into an examining room, where I waited for my breast surgeon to do the first part, something called a wire localization. This technique was used to mark the location of the breast abnormality. My doctor used a guide wire to lead her to the area of the tissue that needed to be removed, where the clip was. She would then work alongside the radiologist to do the lumpectomy.

This first part was what I dreaded the most, and I would be awake for it. It reminded me of the horrific biopsy I'd had done on my breast. You know the one…where I passed out with my boob still in the machine! At least for the lumpectomy, I would be asleep.

Not equipped with the angel worry stone—I was told not to bring any personal belongings with me—I was feeling anxious. Once again, I found myself longing for my mother.

There I sat with Brian in another cold, bleak examining room. If we spoke a few words to each other, that would have been a lot. What more was there to say? It felt like we had both had enough bad news for a lifetime by now, and we were drained.

Brian was allowed to stay with me until they called me into the radiologist's room. We only waited a few minutes before I heard my name called.

"Valerie, you can come on back now." A nurse invited me to follow her down the hall.

"I love you," Brian said, then he drew me in for a tender embrace.

"I love you too," I answered back with my head buried into his strong, firm chest.

Then I walked with the nurse down the hall and went to meet my medical team for the day.

Somebody must have tipped off everyone in the room about what had happened during the biopsy, because once they got started the nurses were constantly asking me if I was doing okay. They softly reminded me to keep breathing.

Breathe, just breathe, Valerie, I said to myself the entire time my breast was being compressed in the mammogram machine. This was reminiscent of that awful day when *both* my breasts were torqued every which way for hours. This time, it would only last about thirty minutes.

Then it hit me. Feasibly, this could be my last mammogram ever. I guessed I should soak it all in.

Just then, I felt a cold drop of liquid on my arm, and when I looked down, I noticed it was my own blood. From that point on, I picked a spot on the wall ahead of me to focus on. I tried to disassociate myself from what was being done to me, and before I knew it, it was done. For thirty minutes I had accepted the fact that I would have to suck it up and be comfortable with being uncomfortable.

Next, I headed over to the preop area for my lumpectomy, where Brian was waiting for me. "You doing okay?" he asked.

"Yeah, it wasn't too bad. I think they are going to take me right in to get my lumpectomy. Are you staying here?" I wanted to be sure he would be there to take me right home; there was no way I was staying any longer than I had to.

"Of course," Brian reassured me as the anesthesiologist walked into the room.

I turned my attention to him. "Hey, I know you!"

He smiled and responded, "Hi, Valerie. If you would prefer, I can find another doctor to be with you during your procedure. But sometimes it's nice to have a familiar face in the room."

"Definitely, I am glad to see you!" I told him. Actually, I felt a sense of relief. He was a member at the gym I managed at the time, where he also attended my spinning classes. It seemed everywhere I went, I would run into someone who knew me from the gym, and examining rooms and hospitals were no exception.

My breast surgeon entered. "Good morning, Valerie. Do you have any last-minute questions for me before we begin?" she asked. I really couldn't think of any. She wrote down Brian's cell phone number and informed him she would call as soon as she was through so he could meet me in the recovery room. She excused herself to allow Brian to wish me well.

"I will see you in a bit. I love you," he said. I returned the same sentiment before I was wheeled into the operating room to have my lumpectomy.

To prep me for surgery, the nurses took each arm and placed them straight out like the letter t. The anesthesiologist then placed an oxygen mask over my nose and mouth while explaining to me that they were ready to start the propofol drip to induce sleeping so they could start the procedure. He asked me to count back from ten, and I think I made it to about eight before I drifted off to sleep.

When I woke up, I heard a nurse call my name. "Valerie… Valerie, you're all done, my dear. Everything went great. I am going to bring you into the recovery room now, okay? Your husband is in there."

"Hey, how'd she do?" he asked the nurse as she wheeled me in, and she reassured him that I did great. She instructed Brian to have me drink some ginger ale very slowly and someone should be in shortly to check on me. When she left I asked Brian for my phone so I could call my sister, who I knew was probably sitting at her work desk, tied to her phone with worry. She always worried about me, and I hated that I caused her to do so.

Since losing our mom just that year, and now my health scare, my sister and I had become closer in a different way. For example, we texted more, just to touch base. She was still in Syracuse, and we saw each other only a few times a year. However, we didn't let a day go by without checking in by text, email, or phone. Sometimes she would send me a simple, "I love you, miss you," and I would be sure to let her know the same. It seemed we were both determined to show our love more. Making a point to never let the other feel alone seemed more crucial since burying our mother. Our mother, who let us both know that was *exactly* how she felt—alone.

I hardly remember what I said to my sister to let her know I did great, but apparently it was enough to convince her, so she told me she would check back in on me the next day.

I stayed in the recovery room until my blood pressure stabilized.

An hour later, Brian helped me into a wheelchair to bring me down to the car, where I apparently decided to call my sister *again*, forgetting that I'd already talked with her in the recovery room. Still weary from the anesthesia, I began to repeat the same information until she interrupted me to say, "I know all of this, Valerie. You don't remember talking to me earlier? Now, go home and get some rest, please." After that, we headed home.

The entire team did a great job. That was the way I viewed everything from that point on: We were a team. The doctors, nurses, technicians, anesthesiologists, and me, all on the same side, each doing his or her part to get to a successful outcome. That day I took on the responsibility of remaining calm and breathing to pull through a very tough procedure without incident. By remembering to breathe, I helped the rest of the team to do their jobs flawlessly.

When we arrived home Brian settled me in, then headed out to get Bailey and Collin from his mom. They had both been in school all day and went straight to Mema's house to do homework and have dinner, which was a huge help, because all I wanted to do was sleep. I was completely wiped out. As tired as I felt, I couldn't wait to see them, so I tried my best to not doze off before they arrived.

It seemed lately all I wanted was my family. Events were so out of the ordinary, leaving a constant feeling of angst inside me, that I hated being alone for too long. I impatiently waited for the kids to arrive to hear all about their day.

Our oldest child, Bailey, knew a little about the procedure I had, but Collin still did not. I continued to tread very lightly as the date of my mastectomy approached. I would use the time to think a little bit more about what I would discuss with both of them, but aware that what I would say to my daughter would be very different from what I would reveal to my son.

When the kids arrived home, Collin ran into my room, hopping up on my bed, with Bailey following close behind.

He caught me up on his day. "Mommy, Mema made chicken casserole and then we got to play cards, and guess what…I won both hands! Can I play for a little more, or do I have to start getting ready for bed?" Collin asked in a sweet enough way for me to respond with permission to stay up a little longer than the normal time.

Meanwhile, Bailey remained quiet. She began to slowly wiggle her way up next to me to find out more about how I was feeling and what "it" was like. We cuddled as I described how quick and fairly painless it was. I told her that Mommy should be much better by tomorrow. Feeling calmer after seeing that I really was okay, she kissed me good night and went off to her room for the evening.

The next day I took it easy, doing light chores around the house, and on the day after that I was able to return to work.

My job as the assistant general manager at a local gym required a fair amount of desk duty, and that I could do. I took a few days off from teaching my group exercise classes, but overall, the recovery from the lumpectomy was not bad at all. Within a few days my Steri-strips fell off and I resumed all normal activities.

A few days after my lumpectomy, a lifelong friend, Kimberly, called. She was aware of everything that had been going on and wanted to check in to see how I was feeling. "Hey, you! So…*how did it go?*" she asked with slight hesitation in her voice, then began to press more. "Seriously, tell me how you're holding up." This time, there was empathy in her tone.

"Pretty good…I don't know, it's just…I guess what I mean is… it's not that I am questioning my decision about the mastectomy; that's not it at all. I'm nervous, but…" Then I stopped talking and began a self-justified pity party. You know the ones. Those pathetic pity parties that you can only invite your true friends to, friends who sometimes know you almost better than you know yourself.

Kimberly was that type of friend to me, so I felt safe enough to continue...

"This isn't *normal*...to remove your boobs!" Out of my mind with grief, anger, and frustration, a barrage of emotions chose that exact moment to smack me in the face. I began to pace back and forth in my kitchen as I let everything I had been feeling as a woman spill out over the phone to another woman I trusted deeply.

"Kimberly, this is just so surreal. I realize what I have to do, but I still can't believe that I am actually having both my tits removed! It's crazy; this whole year has been so fucked up, what the hell? I keep fearing that this will shatter any confidence I have, how could it not? And what the fuck, I mean I just lost my mom! She should be here, this isn't fair, none of this is fair! I have tried so hard to take care of myself. Why is this happening to me?"

Just as I began questioning my own strength to get through what I was about to face, Kimberly gently interrupted me. "Valerie, breathe."

There's that word again, "breathe." Why did I keep forgetting to do something my body should do organically?

Kimberly continued, "I can't imagine what you are feeling, but you will never have to rely on *only* your strength. You have me. I will be here for you. In the meantime, check out this Facebook page. It is full of inspiring women who have gone through mastectomies due to breast cancer or as a preventive."

I halfheartedly agreed to check it out, but thus far the few images I had glanced at online had scared the shit out of me. By now I was also exhausted from reading so much information, so the thought of looking at yet another page dedicated to breast cancer and mastectomies seemed more daunting than helpful.

After the pity party wound down, I began to cry, apologizing to her that I was just tired and overwhelmed. She responded like any great friend would—she cried with me.

Kimberly and I had been friends since elementary school; we had a relationship that was comfortable, one that allowed us to hang out without having to say anything. A friendship that never required us to be entertaining during our visits. Our time did not have to involve fancy get-togethers or best friend necklaces, like the ones our more popular friends wore in junior high. Instead, our friendship had the honor of being invited into the real shit, all of the ugly truths of life. The unpolished, dusty mess of our homes and of ourselves was on full display, without judgment. Ours was a friendship that I had come to cherish more the older I got. One that I trusted and needed now more than ever before.

Yes, I would have the reconstruction. I understood enough about breast reconstruction to know they could do a nice job. But the fact still remained that my body would be very different, and *nothing* about what I was about to do was normal. Frankly, I didn't think I should feel that it *was* normal. What's normal about removing your breasts? Nothing. God gave me my body, and now I was about to fuck with it.

There are no magic words a friend or loved one can tell you to make it okay. All they can do is let you know they are there for you. I knew Kimberly was there for me. In that moment she demonstrated her faith in me was greater than my own in myself. She promised to check in and remind me that everything would turn out great, and if I was experiencing any doubts about that, to please lean on her, she could take it.

By the end of the conversation, Kimberly had me laughing. We began to joke around about the fact that she was the next one to turn forty at the end of the month, on New Year's Eve. She always teased me about being *so* much older than her and that year was no different. In fact, I think it stung a little more now that we would both hit the big 4-0!

Five days after my lumpectomy, my breast surgeon called with the confirmation that it was, in fact, Lobular Carcinoma In Situ. Thankfully, no lymph nodes were involved, and she would see me on December 26, when we would discuss preventive options.

I did not bother repeating to her that my mind was made up. I thought she would still insist on reviewing with me, again, all my options. This was too important of a conversation to have over the phone; it needed to be done in person.

SIX

Holidaze

"I know why families were created with all of their imperfections. They humanize you. They are made to make you forget yourself occasionally, so that the beautiful balance of life is not destroyed."

~ANAIS NIN

CHRISTMAS HAD ALWAYS BEEN A VERY SPECIAL TIME IN my family, and our faith remained the foundation of our holiday celebrations. Despite how difficult 2013 had been, most days I tried my best to keep focused on the good, starting with my faith. In the past it had always helped me to cope. But as hard as I tried, despite the bendable light that Jesus provided me, I was struggling, and continuing to stumble without His light to guide me. Christmas was no different, although being around my family was something I was looking forward to for many reasons; putting my health scare to the side was at the top of my list.

Each year since Brian and I married, we had hosted Christmas Eve dinner at our home for my husband's side of the family and, on Christmas Day, we visited mine. Cooking was not only something I loved to do, I found it very relaxing. The preparations also helped me to keep my mind off my appointment the day after Christmas. Most Christmas Eves, I made lasagna, or something easy enough to keep warm while we were at Mass.

Traditionally, we met up with family at the four o'clock Christmas Eve Mass at Saint Francis Xavier Church. The need to claim our pew was taken very seriously by my family, as this holiday tended to bring out all the usual suspects—the "good" Catholics who hadn't seen the inside of a church likely since the last Christmas Eve. We arrived ninety minutes early to stake our claim and waited for our church choir to begin the beautiful array of religious Christmas songs and hymns, which was always my favorite part.

The choir started with a few songs: "It Came Upon the Midnight Clear," "Angels We Have Heard on High," and "Hark! The Herald Angels Sing." And then they began the first few chords to "Oh Holy Night." It was then that sadness started to creep in. Music has the ability to hit us on such a deep level. I could listen to one song and perceive it one way, and, depending on my mood, another day it would hit me differently. "O Holy Night," which I had always admired for the lovely song it was, evoked such deep feelings of loss for me that night, the first Christmas without my mom.

Softly, I began to cry. Without saying a word, my mother-in-law reached into her purse and handed me a tissue.

A few moments later, Father walked over to say hello. He asked Collin to bring up the baby Jesus statue and place him in the manger during the processional at the beginning of Mass. This would be a *big* job, and I could see Collin was very proud to have been asked to take on such a responsibility. Being the somewhat shy kid he was, as Father explained the directions to him, his little cheeks began to turn bright red. He was getting nervous and Father sensed that, so he asked my daughter and my seventeen-year-old niece, Gabriella, to walk up with Collin during the procession. Both those sweet girls, without hesitation, looked directly at the priest and graciously replied, "No, thank you."

I couldn't believe what I had just heard. Did those little darlings just say no to our priest when he asked them to do a service for the church? What the hell? I mean, what in all that was holy were they thinking? The wrath of the Church had nothing on the wrath they were both going to get from me and my "hairy eyeball" stare as I began to plead through my death stare, all the while hoping that Father wouldn't sense my desperation. *Please...please, take up the baby Jesus! You* will *take up the baby Jesus!* I thought to myself. Maybe if I glared at them long and hard enough, they would succumb to my death stare and mom powers and take up the baby Jesus. *Please, oh please, take up the baby Jesus!*

I got nothing; my powers failed me.

Our priest remained standing right behind me as they continued to refuse. By now I was totally mortified. Father took the hint and mercifully put us all out of our misery. "No problem, girls." With that, I suggested Collin could walk up with a few of the kids from CCD who he knew, and Father agreed.

When it came time, all the children were adorable walking down the aisle, Collin proudly carrying the baby Jesus. Together, the children carefully knelt down and lay him in the manger on the altar. I turned to look at the girls to see if they showed any remorse, but all they seemed to be feeling was relief.

They probably did not want all eyes on them, making them feel more awkward than girls already did at that age.

But it was the comic relief I needed to shake off the feelings of sadness that were attempting to take me over. Later that night we all had a good laugh about how Father was breathing down my neck while I was silently begging the girls to *take the baby Jesus... take him!*

The kids rushed into our bedroom that Christmas morning, just as they did every year, up bright and early, anxious to see what Santa had brought. They were excited for their gifts and equally excited to see if Santa had brought our new dog Sasha anything too. Sasha was a rescue dog we'd brought home the previous year; this was her first Christmas with us.

"Can we start, can we start?" they asked, bursting with anticipation. Half asleep, we gave them the green light to begin with their stockings so we could get our coffee first. Coffee was a must for us to brace for the impending chaos. Santa usually hid their stockings somewhere in their bedrooms, so they ran off to their rooms to search. Casually, Brian and I made our way to the living room, coffee in hand, and watched as Bailey and Collin dumped the contents of their stockings onto the floor.

"Santa knows we have Sasha now, Mom!" Collin shouted out. "Look, there's a stocking for her too!"

With our respective places taken on the couch, the tearing of the wrapping paper commenced. The magic of Christmas when the kids were little didn't just exist in the presents. It was in everything around us. The lights, the music, the way we all laughed together during the same moments of the same repeated holiday movies. It was in the smells that came from my kitchen, a kitchen that seemed so much warmer during the holidays, as did our home. As cozy as we wanted to remain there all day, our next stop was my grandmother's house.

It was sure to be a very difficult time for all, especially for my grandmother. I may have lost my mom, but she'd lost her daughter, and that was a pain no mother should ever have to bear. My aunts and cousins would also be there. My sister and her family were unable to come down to Connecticut during the winter; she remained up in Syracuse. That first Christmas without my mother made me miss my sister during all the "firsts" without her.

Secretly, my sister and I shared the burden of knowing how our mom, at the young age of fifty-nine, *really* died. Not in her sleep, as we'd told our grandmother. Not peacefully, and not with anyone by her side. No one was with her, because she'd refused to let us, or anyone else, in. Instead, she'd put on the fake mask of pretending everything was fine. Anytime you asked my mother how she was, that was her answer: "I'm fine." Then she would quickly turn the focus back onto whomever or whatever else she could. She was a master of the art of deflection. I began to hate the word "fine."

The irony was not lost on me that we were now left to do the same thing for the sake of others, pretend that everything was okay when it was far from it.

My family had a very proficient skill set when it came to shoving all the uncomfortable subjects way down. Bury them deep, so they may never have a chance of rising to the surface to be discussed. Therefore, the subject of anything to do with my mom was sure to *not* be discussed that Christmas at Gram's house.

None of us were ready to break out the family photo albums and reminisce over the happier times anyhow. It was way too raw, and exceedingly painful. Hell, I still couldn't bring myself to look at an image of my mother without feeling immense torment that I was unable to sort through. So, I didn't. Instead, I allowed my grandmother's albums to collect another layer of dust before I was ready to peek inside. I felt like I was doing the same for my soul, letting it slowly collect dust.

Because no one at my grandmother's house was ready to flip through those pages of happier times, we considerately acknowledged the depth of loss felt by everyone. In some ways that in and of itself was comforting, just in a really fucked up way. But that was family: messy and complicated. And mine was no different from anyone else's.

Grief is a funny animal. Everyone certainly experiences it differently. One thing I knew about this animal so far: Just when I thought it was through with me, it sank its teeth in deeper.

Although my sister couldn't be with us, she'd sent her presents ahead of time but asked me to wait until she phoned to open mine.

When my grandmother's phone rang, I ran to answer it. Monica was on the other end. "Open it…open it!" she insisted. It was a single envelope that I ripped open, finding a letter describing her family's very generous gift of a trip for me to go see my nephew run at Nationals in Portland, Oregon, the next year!

I was totally floored, amazed that she'd done this for me. She wanted me to have something to look forward to, knowing all I was about to face. My nephew was in high school and a very gifted athlete who ran with a nationally recognized cross-country team. They usually made it to Nike Cross Nationals in Oregon every year. The following year he would be a senior; it would be his last year with the team. Whenever his team was close enough for me to see him race, the kids and I tried our best to go watch him. My sister knew how badly I wanted to see him run in Oregon, so she'd made that possible with her gift. I was elated! To be honest, I think that moment was the closest I had come to really smiling about anything in what seemed like forever. Finally, something positive to look forward to!

In 2008, we began celebrating Christmas in my grandmother's tiny and very cozy senior living apartment. Before then, we had big family gatherings in her four-bedroom ranch-style home. That home had a large finished basement that was perfect for family celebrations. There was a time that basement also served as a temporary apartment for my mom and me when I was in my early twenties. My mom was forty at that time, the same age I was when I lost her.

Reflecting back, those were chaotic days. My mother was drinking heavily and added whatever pills she could to mask her pain—and none of it was regulated. Doctors were more lenient about phoning in just about anything you asked for, and monitoring the use of those pills was also very lax. My mother worked in a medical office and befriended a doctor who liked his prescription pad almost as much as he liked her. I didn't mind my mother's lonely nights of drinking then; it kept her off my back. It also gave me the freedom to do a fair amount of reckless partying myself. Little did I know that the partying I would do in my twenties would set me up for a long and laborious tiptoe down the path of addiction to alcohol myself.

After my mother died, I wasn't drinking. I also wanted to remain as physically healthy as possible going into a major surgery.

Sitting in my grandmother's teeny apartment, without a drop of alcohol in me, left me empty. Other than that brief moment of joy from Monica's gift, I felt completely hollow. Dusty like the albums I refused to look at. Why couldn't I just get on with life, open the family photo albums and reminisce, like a *normal* person?

My grandparents had moved from Syracuse to retire in the quaint New England town of New Milford, Connecticut, in 1982 My grandfather was a little man in stature but firm in his nature, earning him the nickname "Little Big Daddy." Our Little Big Daddy who loved the Red Sox. I can still remember his smell to this day. Yes, everyone has a distinct smell. His was coffee; my mother's was lavender.

My grandfather was diagnosed with type I diabetes at the age of four. In his day, if you had that, the doctors didn't hold out very much hope that you would go on to live a long life, father children, or do half the things he would go on to do. My grandparents were high school sweethearts. They grew up in the very small town of Dover, New York. There, he was raised on a farm where his mother took impeccable care of him. She needed to be very diligent about what he ate and when he ate it. My great-grandmother must have been very relieved when her son met and fell in love with my grandmother. You see, my grandmother was headed to college to study nursing. I am sure it gave my great-grandmother such comfort, knowing her son would be in good hands, married to a nurse, although that almost wasn't the case.

When my grandfather first asked my grandmother to be his date to a school dance, she declined. She knew who he was, that he excelled in academics and played sports like baseball and hockey, but she wasn't interested in him. Luckily, she decided to meet him at the dance anyhow, which gave him the opportunity to work his schoolboy charm on her, and they began dating. When they both graduated from Dover High School, he was the valedictorian of their class. He earned a scholarship to a college in Schenectady, New York, but became ill and had to return home. He tried attending the Pratt Institute for Engineering, but once again his health became an issue. He never gave up. He persevered and studied accounting at a small business school, where he earned his degree.

My grandmother went on to college for nursing in Long Island. She did most of her training in New York City. They continued dating and planned to marry. They were engaged in 1948 and married on May 22, 1949. My grandmother, Marie Feathers, became Marie Darling. Before settling down to have children, my grandmother worked at Sharon Hospital in Connecticut and did some private-duty jobs as well. My grandfather worked as a tax accountant for a large agricultural company, where he was recognized for his abilities and promoted to their company headquarters in Syracuse. There, they raised four children—three girls and one boy—Sheryl, Bev, Donna, and William (Billy). My grandmother put her career as a nurse on hold to take care of her children and her husband. I am convinced it was because of her love and attention to what he needed that he was able to do the things he loved and lived as long as he did.

They always knew that when he retired at the young age of fifty-five, they would move closer to their roots, closer to Dover. That was where they came across New Milford, just over the New York border, where he and my grandmother moved to their new four-bedroom ranch.

In the summer of 1994, my grandfather fell very ill. I was just leaving a two-year college where I barely attended class, was totally unfocused, and not quite sure of where I was going next. I knew my grandmother needed help taking care of my grandfather, and I needed someplace new to go. I left Syracuse at the ripe age of twenty with no commitments and no plans other than to help my grandmother, crash with my mom in my grandparents' basement, and get temporary work for the summer. I took one job waitressing and two others part-time—working the front desk at a health club that had just opened and as an outdoor adventure instructor. All of my "professions" at that point came from meeting the right people at the right time. For example, I got my job as an outdoor adventure instructor when a really cool and charming guy came in to the health club and asked if I had any interest in becoming a rock-climbing instructor. Pretty random, and I had no idea why he asked me other than perhaps he thought I was cute; he certainly liked talking with me when he came into the gym.

Growing up in a fairly suburban area, my only real experience with the outdoors was when my friends and I purposely got lost in a very small section of woods. It was the type of place that, if you were truly lost and screamed for help, someone in the adjacent neighborhoods would hear you.

Now here I was in Connecticut, in a place far from what I had ever known, looking for something to do with myself. I figured learning to be a climbing instructor would be a great new adventure, so I said yes to the job. I learned many outdoor skills beyond rock climbing. It was also then that I fell in love with being outdoors, inspiring people to test their limits and find what fueled their souls. Summer turned to fall, then winter, and I never went back to Syracuse. Looking back now, I realize those were some of the best years of my life—chaos and all—*but at least I felt it.*

During that time, I worked as much as I could, spent time with my family, and met new friends. One day I was working one of my many jobs, at a restaurant, and received a call from my aunt Donna. She informed me that hospice was at Grandma's house. She said my grandfather didn't have much longer now and that I should come home.

I arrived at my grandmother's house to see my Little Big Daddy in his makeshift hospital bed that was set up for him in the living room. He was partially sedated to make him comfortable, but I knew he could still feel and hear us.

The room was quiet except for the occasional whisper. We each took turns holding his hand, telling him we loved him. My grandmother was the last to hold his hand as he drifted away. With family surrounding his bedside, he died with a smile on his face…a smile. He was only sixty-nine. It was such a surreal moment in time when I felt sadness and peace all at once. The first and only time I had witnessed someone passing on to eternity, proving by his expression heaven must exist.

That time in my life brought me even closer to my grandmother. I continued to live with her until I met Brian, almost four years later, at the same restaurant I started working at when I first moved to Connecticut.

The home where my grandfather took his last breath was no longer ours to celebrate in, but some traditions carried on. Like always going to Grandmother's house for the holidays, no matter how tiny or overheated it was. From the look on my husband's and son's faces, I'd guess it was a balmy eighty-five degrees in there that day. I spied the little crack in the sliding glass door that Brian had opened, trying desperately not to sweat through his brand-new and very itchy wool Christmas sweater. Both my boys anxiously awaited the properly portioned meal they were about to receive, rationed out just as my grandmother was used to doing, having grown up during the Great Depression.

Even with all that, Christmas just felt *right* at Grandma's house, especially that year. Without my mom, I thought as long as we were all together, in any space, eating whatever food, and even dying a slow and painful death by heatstroke, we would be just fine.

We individually went on to carry the burden of our unspoken grief.

SEVEN

Decisions, Decisions...

*"A wise man makes his own decisions.
An ignorant man follows public opinion."*

~**Chinese Proverb**

THE DAY AFTER CHRISTMAS ALL I WANTED WAS TO EAT leftovers and stay in my jammies all day. Instead, I needed to get my ass in gear and get ready to meet with my breast surgeon to discuss my lumpectomy results and treatment options. I'd learned a few things about this doctor from just meeting her a couple of times. She was very knowledgeable, well-prepared, and organized; however, she did not have the most comforting bedside manner. But what I would need her for, to be honest, didn't require a warm bedside manner. She would be doing the breast removal. But for the reconstruction part, I wanted to be sure I had a doctor I connected with. I would have many appointments throughout that phase with the plastic surgeon.

There was just something about my breast surgeon, though, that made me feel almost scared to tell her I had made up my mind to go ahead with the preventive mastectomy. Maybe it was the shame I'd started putting on myself, feeling my issues were so much *less than* what other women were or had gone through, fully aware of the fact that every day she dealt with women who were fighting to live. My decision was a preventive measure, not life or death. My news from the cancer world was considered a relief, even by me.

We began by discussing the results of the lumpectomy, the same news she had already given me over the phone, when she asked me if I was still considering the bilateral mastectomy with reconstruction, I answered, yes, I was. She did not discuss what the procedure would be like, or the recovery; in a matter-of-fact way she told me we would do that at a later date. Her voice was always a monotone when she spoke with me, and each time she introduced new information, she made sure I understood what she'd just said by confirming, "Does this make sense?" Most times I did understand, and when I did not, I knew I could always call the breast surgery navigator, who was more approachable to me. The navigator worked in the same office and was available for patients to explain the nonsurgical details. Details such as what bras you may want to wear postsurgery or what comforts to have at home while you are recovering. The navigator had a much softer way about her.

We wrapped up the appointment, and the surgeon gave me two referrals for a plastic surgeon. The first was the one I was hoping she would refer me to. The second one specialized in the TRAM flap reconstructive option.

The thought of having more scars on my body was not at all appealing to me, which would happen with the TRAM flap option, a procedure essentially using fat, skin, and muscle from your lower abdomen in your reconstruction. My thyroid cancer surgery had left a scar on my neck, so I had some idea of what the scars across my new, reconstructed breast could look like. So the TRAM flap option, for me, just didn't feel right. I quickly ruled it out.

After I left the breast surgeon's office, I immediately called my friend Molly, who'd had a preventive bilateral mastectomy with reconstruction earlier in 2013. She invited me over so I could ask her some questions. We sat together on her couch as she opened herself up. Mostly I wanted her to go over with me what the surgery itself was like, and the recovery. How long was it before she was able to get back to exercising? She offered a lot of helpful information, answering all my questions and bringing up things I hadn't even thought about. Things like how Brian was going to have to be around to help, or someone was, especially in the first week or so, when I would still have the drains in. Molly and I were both very active people, with young kids who had equally active academic and social lives. She understood my concerns about being laid up, not able to work out the way I was used to. In fact, she told me I wouldn't be able to do that for a long time. She asked if I had given any thought to who would help with the kids, and *really* stressed the importance of having someone around to help in the beginning. I asked her what the removal of her breasts was like, how the expanders felt in her chest, and, overall, how all of it made her *feel*. I wanted to know how it impacted how she felt as a woman, and if it affected her self-confidence or -worth. But I didn't have the courage. We went over a lot of details—medical, logistical, and others—but we never addressed whether her mastectomy had affected her spirit.

Even though I lacked the courage to ask Molly the questions that were weighing like a heavy blanket on my mind, I did take tremendous comfort in being able to use her as a positive example that everything would be okay. I knew that when it came time to tell Bailey what was going on with me, I could use Molly's story to calm any uncertainties she may have. Molly would provide a great frame of reference for my daughter.

After we wrapped up our question-and-answer session, Molly asked if I wanted to see her breasts. "I'm okay with it if you are," I said to her, especially curious because she'd used the same plastic surgeon I was hoping to see; of course I wanted to see his fine work! Up until this point, the only breast reconstruction surgeries I had seen were in the photos I struck up enough courage to glance at on the Internet and, truthfully, they mostly scared the shit out of me.

Molly sat across from me on the couch and lifted up her blouse. I didn't know what to say. Her breasts looked better than I had anticipated, but still not like real or natural breasts, or even the ones from a boob job. Don't get me wrong…she looked amazing, just not what I was picturing at first. In fact, I don't know exactly what I had anticipated. Her scarring, her tattooed nipples—I didn't realize they could even tattoo nipples on! In that moment, I discovered I didn't know very much at all about what breast reconstruction looked like. I asked her about her nipples, and she told me the doctor would explain all my options when it was time for that. She summed it up by saying, "It's basically deciding for yourself if you prefer lights on all the time or lights off." Also, she disclosed that reconstructing a nipple required more procedures, and she'd decided she was done with surgeries, so the tattoos were a good option for her. Molly got up from the couch before she continued. "I mean, let's be honest, up close you can obviously tell they aren't real, but from far away, you really can't." She walked to the other side of the room to prove her point.

She looked beautiful, vulnerable, and strong, all at the same time. Opening herself up like that to me so I could feel better about what the process would be like was incredibly brave.

I'd had no idea all my friend had been through until we talked. No idea at all, and, frankly, I felt ashamed and embarrassed that I hadn't offered her more help during her recovery. If I'd known, I would have been there.

Before Molly put her shirt back on, she asked if I wanted to feel her breasts. "Go ahead, touch them. They feel great, even though I can't sense you touching them!" That too never occurred to me—how much sensation I would lose. Embarrassed but curious at the same time, I touched her breasts. They felt soft and very real; again, not what I was expecting. She reassured me that she looked and felt great in clothes, but being naked took getting used to. However, she was eight months postsurgery and very happy with her decision.

The grace Molly showed me that evening was so selfless, something I am eternally grateful for.

Before I left, she offered to go with me when I had my consultation with the plastic surgeon, and I took her up on it. She also made one last point, letting me know this would not be an easy recovery. It would take time and I would need to do my best to remain positive. Molly also made me aware of some of the ignorant comments that may come my way from people who just did not understand why a woman would choose to have a preventive mastectomy. She shared some of the cruel remarks she had endured, like, "You're so lucky, you'll have a brand-new set of boobs when this is said and done!"

Molly's reminder to keep my loved ones—those who truly support me—close, did not come as a shock. By this time, a few comments already were being made about me—gossip at work and in larger "friend" circles—that were very insensitive. I had to remind myself that some people may just be uniformed, and at that time, I did not have the energy to educate them. Then there were the others, the cruel and heartless ones who said horrible things, like, "She is probably doing this for the boob job," or "At least it's not cancer." Well, those hurt more than I ever let on. I did my best not to give those people any more of my energy. In doing so, some minor adjustments were made in my "friend" group. The only opinion that truly mattered on this subject was my own.

I don't need my boobs to live. Every time I was feeling scared, I would return to my newfound, twisted mantra: *I don't need my boobs to live.*

A few days later Molly and I met with the plastic surgeon. The three of us sat together in the examining room, and I was once again asked if I understood my diagnosis and treatment options. I assured him I did. I explained my reasons for choosing to have this surgery. He did not question it and got right to his examination, asking me, "Valerie, have you thought about the size?"

"A size?" I was taken aback. I don't know why, but of all the things I had considered, I hadn't given much thought to what size I wanted to be. "Not really. I just want to be the way I am now." He lifted up my little boobies a bit higher and said, "Maybe more like this?"

Okay, so perhaps gravity had taken over a bit, but hey, I had just turned forty, give a girl a break!

He explained that my next step was to see a genetic counselor at the hospital. He assured me it was all part of the process and not to worry. I returned home to make the phone call for that appointment to get it taken care of right away.

I was able to get an appointment with a genetic counselor three weeks later. I had been to counselors before, but never one for my genes! I also had another follow-up with my breast surgeon on the same day to discuss the operation in greater detail.

The meeting with the genetic counselor was to review my personal and family history. Prior to arriving, I had to fill out four pages of paperwork, answering extensive questions about my health history as well as my family's. I was a bit embarrassed to hand it in only half completed because I knew nothing about my biological father or his family.

I learned about genetic testing options, or if I even needed to be tested at all. I was not really familiar with this subject other than brief tidbits I had heard in the news, but it seemed to be a hot topic at the time. Recently women were being tested to see if they carried the BRCA1 and/or BRCA2 genes, which could put them at risk for breast and ovarian cancer.

In the waiting room I repeated all the same mind-occupying activities I had become so accustomed to indulging in until my name was called. Noticing young couples, some expecting, some with babies, coming in and out of the waiting room, I thought to myself, *Please, God, I pray this isn't a young family battling cancer and now the mother is here for genetic testing too.* I later learned that in that office, along with genetic counseling, they also took care of high-risk pregnancies—women who are fighting cancer while pregnant, gestational cancers. Every time I heard of someone else's struggles or learned new things like that, it would snap everything right back into perspective for me. I was fighting for my health, not my life, and certainly not for the life of a baby inside me like the women I saw in that waiting room were. You know that old saying, "If everyone placed all their problems in the center of the table, you'd take back your own"? I felt that deeply.

The meeting with the genetic counselor was brief. She asked me some of the questions that were on the paperwork I had already filled out. When it came to the lack of information for my father's side of the family, she seemed unfazed. She began to draw a makeshift family tree on a piece of paper and explained that it helped her to see any patterns she needed to be looking for. We went over the fact that my maternal side of the family had several random but seemingly genetically unlinked cancers, and, in my case, it really didn't matter anyway since LCIS is not thought to be genetically linked. In fact, some studies suggest that less than 10 percent of breast cancers are hereditary. I would later call my sister to tell her she was safe; as usual, I was the only one who was fucked up. Thankfully, there would be no need for her to contact a genetic counselor herself. It was a huge relief to learn that this did not have to concern my sister or my daughter, healthwise at least. The genetic counselor told me there was no need for me to be tested and wished me luck with everything.

Later in the day I headed to my breast surgeon's office filled with angst about having a conversation about my decision. Not because I was still questioning it, but because I felt, from the very beginning, this particular doctor would rather me stop at the lumpectomy and go the medicine-and-scanning route with close monitoring. Hers was, in fact, the most conservative of the three opinions I sought, but she was the most experienced.

My feelings were confirmed when, during our appointment, she began to lecture me on all the possible "what-ifs" that may happen during a major surgery like a mastectomy. I realized she was just doing her job, but her speech went, for the first time, from monotone to harsh. And she constantly repeated the word "prophylactic."

"Valerie, this is considered a prophylactic mastectomy—a method used only to reduce your risk of breast cancer," the doctor stated.

Eww. I hated that word, *prophylactic*. It made me think of a condom. I always referred to it as a preventive mastectomy. She continued to try to drill into my head that just because I was at high risk of developing cancer, it didn't mean I would. She also told me that I would never fully regain the strength in my chest muscles. She realized my level of activity, the fact that I loved to race—running, biking, and, most recently, triathlons—the fact that my job required me to be physically fit; she was acutely aware of all this.

We touched on the history of anxiety and depression in my family and how, at times, I had my own struggles with both.

"You should know that a lot of women experience anxiety or

depression after having a mastectomy, even with the reconstruction," she said. "They really struggle with body image, and I just don't want you to have this done and regret it five, ten years from now. Implants shift, especially in active women. I can't tell you how many times I have had women come back into my office wishing they never had the surgery in the first place." It was then she reassured me that this wasn't her personal opinion, although I believed in my heart it was. She was just taking one more opportunity to go over my options.

She added, "You can always change your mind…even the day of the surgery." Now her voice was the same as always—steady, with no inflection. Her eyes, however, were caring, and for the first time I felt some compassion from her. I actually empathized with *her* a little, my surgeon—a woman my age who would remove my breasts. They say doctors try not to get emotionally involved, but her eyes were telling me something different. She may have known more, medically speaking—about the scans, the drugs, all the modern-day preventive measures they could use to keep a close eye on me—but I knew myself. I knew that it would have been a constant concern of mine, and the thought of always having that "monkey on my back" was too overwhelming. I wanted to get this done and move on with my life, for me and for my family.

I also did my own fair share of reading, and everything I read agreed that a prophylactic mastectomy reduced the risk of developing breast cancer by 90 percent in high-risk women. Women like me, with LCIS, had a 30 to 40 percent higher chance than average women of developing an invasive breast cancer. Besides, I had my new, twisted mantra: *I don't need my boobs to live.* They could take them if doing so increased my chances of not developing breast cancer. At the end of the day, for me, peace of mind won over any statistic I read or the doctor could recite to me.

The surgery was set for February 11, 2014. Before leaving her office, the surgeon added again, "Remember, you can always take more time to think, and don't be afraid to cancel the procedure, even the morning of."

I guess I didn't realize what a controversial or aggressive move I was making. The fact was some surgeons did consider this to be an overly aggressive choice. But the choice was mine to make, and I stood firm, knowing this was the right thing for me. It was time to stop asking for opinions and start preparing myself and my family for my surgery.

EIGHT

Telling the Family

"I you, me too, and that means, I love you."

~GRANDMA DARLING

KIDS KNOW MORE THAN WE GIVE THEM CREDIT FOR. AS parents, we try to talk in codes, omit words, or speak quietly where we hope we will be out of earshot. But it was as if my kids had a built-in radar system that detected whenever we tried to keep anything from them.

Bailey knew about the lumpectomy. She understood they'd found a section in my breast that they were concerned about, so they wanted to remove it. She did *not* know about the mastectomy. I needed to tell her. She was a wise young lady who could handle so much more than I gave her credit for, especially because she herself knew what it was like to have to undergo major surgery.

In October 2011, Bailey was diagnosed with avascular necrosis of the first metatarsal. We were unaware of the fact that her right big toe was slowly dying, until she actually broke it one day at dance practice. It wasn't until she was taking forever to heal that we realized something else was going on.

We were led to a foot specialist who ordered a bone scan, which revealed the avascular necrosis of the grand toe. She had an extensive surgery during which the surgeon had to expand out the joint and hold it in place by using an external fixation device. She had an open wound around the surgical area and wore the device for about eight weeks to allow the fracture to heal and the new space the surgeon expanded out to settle in place. It was considered an idiopathic avascular necrosis, meaning they had no idea how something like that could happen to such a young girl. It was so rare that she was taken on as a case study by a surgeon from the Hospital for Special Surgery in New York City. Bailey had a year of physical therapy—a full year away from what she loved, her passion, dancing, and two months of homeschooling.

I can remember the night we brought her home after her foot surgery, when the nerve blocker wore off. She was in excruciating pain, and I held her all night. She nodded on and off into sleep, and when she wasn't sleeping, she just whimpered. The medicine they sent her home with made her nauseous. There was nothing I could do for her, just hold her. By the next morning things started to get better, as they slowly continued to do over the course of the next year.

I look back at that time and all Bailey had to go through and wonder if I could have handled what she did with such grace. She handled the pain, the frustration of being away from her friends at dance, all of it, like a warrior.

I planned the conversation I was about to have with Bailey ahead of time. I wanted to avoid the word "cancer" as much as possible. Instead, I wanted to be sure she was clear about why I was having this operation. I needed her to know that, for me, for my own emotional well-being, as well as my physical well-being, this was the right choice.

I asked Bailey to come into my bedroom so we could talk. The first thing she said was, "What did I do?"

"Nothing," I assured her. "I need to tell you something important, in private."

She joined me in my room, and we both sat down on the edge of the bed. "Bailey, when I had my lumpectomy, it was because of what was shown on previous tests. The testing showed I *may* be at more of a risk than the average woman for developing breast cancer. I do *not* have it, but one of my options to minimize ever getting it would is to have the same procedure Molly had. Do you remember what she had done?"

"Yes, a mast...something," Bailey responded, with an answer close enough for me to be sure she knew what I was referring to.

We kept the conversation between us honest and uncomplicated. She was fourteen, a young lady whose own body was developing and changing. I did not want her to worry about whether this could happen to her too. I shared with her that I had gone to a specialist who'd explained to me that LCIS was not hereditary and, hopefully, not something she should ever have to worry about herself.

I explained that the surgery would mean I would be recovering at home and there would be some significant time when, physically, I wouldn't be able to do a lot of the things I normally did. I asked if she would be willing to step up and help out with some things around the house. Things like the laundry, the dishes, and helping with her brother.

"Yes!" she quickly reacted. "I can totally cook dinner, and Collin can do the dishes!" She already knew how to delegate like a good big sister should. I also think it made her feel good to have something special to look forward to—planning the meals and taking on more responsibility.

I reassured her that other people would be here for us as well—lots of friends had offered to pitch in. I ended the conversation by asking her if she had any questions, and she asked, "How big are your boobs going to be?"

We both burst out laughing, and I explained, "Like they are now, but maybe just a little higher. You see, gravity takes over and it's comin' for ya too!" She hated when I said that. In certain situations, like when I was changing clothes or we were talking about exercise, I would throw out a little self-deprecating humor and say that same thing, "Gravity...it's comin' for ya!"

It all stemmed from a story about when she was little. I would describe our household as pretty open. We are not a family that is discreet when it comes to changing clothes or getting in or out of the shower, etc., probably because we lived in a modest home, all sharing the same bathroom, so discretion was a difficult thing to have.

When Bailey was about five years old she came into the bathroom to talk with me. I stepped out of the shower, and she looked up at me and said, "Are mine going to be like that someday?"

"Like what?" I replied.

"Long," she answered. She was asking about my breasts!

Starting at a young age, we always had open and honest conversations when our kids had questions, and talking about my mastectomy was just another one of our talks that would draw us closer together and strengthen our bond. I thought of everything we did, about our family, as part of a team. We were determined to get through this bump in the road as any strong team would, by working together and by talking, a far cry from the childhood of secrets I was raised in.

Telling my grandmother was going to be hard. At eighty-six, she had been through so much. She'd buried her husband and lost her son, my uncle, when he was only thirty-seven. For God's sake, the poor woman just laid her eldest daughter to rest. She had been through an enormous amount of pain and loss. Parents should never outlive their children—it's not the normal order of things, at any age. The sorrow she had faced in her lifetime was immeasurable. I couldn't help but feel a bit guilty for adding any more worry or sadness to her life; it weighed on me enormously.

I decided to go to her house and tell her in person. My grandmother was having a very hard time hearing, although she would never admit it. It had gotten so bad that Monica had started a tradition: She, my grandmother, and I would email one another every morning to say hello and catch up on the day's events. We emailed every day, without fail. It was a simple, easy way to stay connected. I also think my grandmother's vision was going, as her emails were always typed in all caps. Either that or she was yelling at us via email…could be!

I walked into her apartment to a delicious smell. She had just put a lemon cake into the oven with eight minutes left to bake, and she asked, "Valerie, do me a favor, would ya? Pay attention and listen for the buzzer. I can't hear that damn thing."

"Yes, Gram." *The woman who insisted she had no problem hearing had asked me for this favor!*

I decided to wait the eight minutes or so before I brought anything up. I didn't want to be interrupted. When the buzzer went off, I pulled the cake out to cool and returned to the living room. As a woman who'd been a nurse, she understood everything as I explained it, and she agreed I was doing the right thing. She even said that if I didn't do this surgery, she would worry about me. Still, her weary face failed to hide her sadness for what I was about to face. My grandmother was heartbroken for me as a woman, and I could see that in her hazel eyes. She may have been hard of hearing, but her eyes never failed her. She could see through it all, even the fortitude I was trying to display for her.

A woman of her grit knew all too well what it was like to put on a brave face for the sake of others, and I couldn't bear to see her sad any longer. I needed to steer the conversation to a lighter note. "Hey, Gram, I asked the doctor to give me boobs like yours," I said.

To that, she replied, "Why the hell would you want to do that? I think mine are in a race to see which one will reach my navel first!"

My grandmother, quick as a whip and sharp as a tack. She had great faith that I would be okay, and when I left, she squeezed me tight and told me with confidence, "If anyone can handle this, kid, it would be you."

"I you, me too, Gram." To us, that meant, "I love you too."

NINE

Preparing for Success

"Give me six hours to chop down a tree and I will spend the first four sharpening the axe."

~ABRAHAM LINCOLN

JUST A FEW SHORT WEEKS AWAY FROM MY SURGERY DATE, and something was kicking my ass. I was pretty sure it was a sinus infection. I'd become susceptible to them, and now I lined up my arsenal of homeopathic remedies, but nothing seemed to be doing the trick. Ugh! I hadn't been sick all winter, and I certainly couldn't afford to be now. The last thing I needed was to have the surgery date postponed by a stupid cold.

Thankfully, I had an appointment with my plastic surgeon, so I headed there to ask him if my operation would have to be put off if I remained sick.

When I arrived at his office, I refilled out the same sort of paperwork I was accustomed to—listing my primary care doctor, any changes in health history or medications, etc. It also asked how I was feeling that day, to which I wanted to respond, "Like shit." Instead, I left it blank, figuring I could review that with him later.

Moments later, "Valerie?" A little drop of sunshine called my name. I looked up and saw a petite blonde, I'd say in her midfifties. She introduced herself as the nurse, and we continued our conversation, during which she found the time to share a wealth of random personal facts, down the hall and into the examining room. We reviewed together some basic pre- and postop information and had ourselves a little "girl talk," as she put it. I also learned more about the two drains that would be in me, how to empty them, and approximately when they would come out—in seven to ten days. She reminded me that I needed to be careful not to lift my arms over my head for at least the first three weeks and, after that, not to lift anything weighing over five pounds for about six weeks.

Of course my immediate thoughts went to what I *could* do. I began envisioning myself back at the gym, riding the recumbent bike and walking on the treadmill, maybe even some light bodyweight exercises with the TRX by week three. I'd already set up my road bike on the trainer in my bedroom, where I would be forced to see it first thing in the morning to remind myself of what I ultimately wanted to get back to: riding it and running outside. Even though cycling and running were hobbies for me, they had also become deep passions.

I actually wasn't much of a runner growing up. I'd picked it up when I first moved to Connecticut in my early twenties. I didn't know anyone in the area and didn't know the area itself, so I would strap on my sneakers and head out the front door of my grandparents' home to investigate my surroundings. What I also discovered was that I reveled in the feeling running gave me.

There was something about the awareness of my feet hitting the pavement. The moving meditation of listening to the rhythm of my pace, albeit slow at first, was therapeutic. Literally putting one foot in front of the other helped to calm my anxious mind, giving me one simple thing to focus on, which was, *just keep going.*

Throughout that time, I ran mostly local road races—everything from a 5K to marathon distance. Racing was fun, of course, but all the training that led up to the racing was what I loved the most. Setting new goals for myself and accomplishing them was important to me. The strong bonds and camaraderie established between training partners and in groups lifted me up, physically and spiritually. In my midtwenties I took my hobby and turned it into a profession. Using my credentials as a personal trainer and group fitness instructor, I started coaching a local community running group. That group evolved into what is known today as the CORE Fitness Method, a group of dedicated peeps who share a passion for discovering their CORE reasons for choosing to make fitness a priority in their lives. These CORE peeps come from all walks of life, with varying levels of fitness and backstories. Stories that include wanting to lose weight for a special event and regaining confidence after a divorce. Some stories were harder than others, like surviving the loss of a child. The simple commitment of being accountable to another person, or group of people, gave them the opportunity to get their power back. And when they did, they paid it forward by helping those around them who needed it, in- and outside of our CORE Group.

The distinct honor of coaching, of being invited to each of these individuals lives, was never lost on me. For decades I coached this group. It would be this group that, unbeknownst to them, would turn out to do the very same for me. To hold me up when I was barely hanging on.

I kept a pretty good ten-year streak, until running began taking a toll on my body. So in my early thirties I added in outdoor cycling and quickly developed a passion for that as well. Whether it was going for group rides for fun or to take in the scenery and stop for a coffee along the route, I cherished my time on the road. Descending a long, gradual hill made me feel free. The challenge of a long, steep uphill climb was something I welcomed. Presenting something to overcome was almost a dare to me. Just dare me to do it and watch me overcome whatever obstacle you throw in my way.

I don't think it was ever out of a sense of feeling overconfident that I tried to conquer different physical challenges; it was quite the opposite in fact. Maybe it was my lack of self-esteem that fueled me to push myself. Whatever it was, it worked for me, and I knew I had to be able to get back to that as quickly as possible after the mastectomy and reconstruction. It was my spiritual practice, one that I was not willing to give up for any reason—a nonnegotiable.

I was aware that my recovery was going to be a long road with rolling hills. But just as I had learned from all those years of endurance training, as long as I kept moving forward, I would overcome this too.

Words I penned for the local running group I coached, the CORE Fitness Method:

I Run For Not From

I run for my health, my freedom and promise,
I run for hope and for the light shone upon us,
I run for the simple feeling it gives me inside,
to trample the dust and let my heart be my guide.

I run for the challenge, to see what I am made of,
I run for my family, my friendships and to show love,
I run through pain, against pain and at times because of it,
I run to beat cancer, for control or lack of it.

I run for vanity, for myself and for stillness,
I run to meet things head on and sometimes for avoidance,
I run for charity, for gratitude and celebration.
I run to stay focused, to divert from temptation.
I run to create memories, moments and laughter,
I run because it gives me so much of what I am after,
I run to inspire to set a good example for my children,
I run to prove your greatest strength comes from within.

I run for many reasons, some of which I can't explain,
*I run because I can, and it will **NEVER** be in vain.*

After we discussed my restrictions, the nurse moved on to explain the scarring. I had seen Molly's and some photos, but when we began to talk about the scars I would be left with, I felt my heart fall to my stomach. From the lumpectomy, my left breast already had a pretty significant scar that ran diagonally across the top. The nurse tried her best to comfort me by telling me that when the breast surgeon went in for the bilateral mastectomy, she might just follow that incision line, and the plastic surgeon would do his best to follow her "lines" thereafter. I shared with her my concerns that if she did follow that line, the scar would be much higher than the one across my right breast. She agreed and said I needed to speak with the plastic surgeon about that valid point.

The nurse went on to explain what the tissue expanders would be like—the hardware that would rebuild my chest to make room for my implants. "Now, what about your nipples, have you made that decision?" she asked.

"I'm not keeping them." My answer was almost as short and sweet as she was.

After our "girl talk" she asked in a very soft voice, "Valerie, I am going to need to take some 'before' photos. Is that okay with you?

If so, I will need you to sign a release form. Sometimes we use these images to show other patients the 'before' and 'after,' omitting your face of course."

I nodded. "Where do you need me to stand?"

As I stood there, still as can be, posing for my "before" photos, I thought to myself, *How is this even real? How the fuck is this me standing here, having my photo taken so another woman who is about to undergo the same thing can make decisions she doesn't want to make about her body?* I sucked in my slightly bloated belly to display my abs, and the nurse laughed and said, "Honey, you can breathe!" Hell no! Hundreds of people would be seeing me—well, from the neck down anyway. I worked hard for my abs, damn it; I was going to let them show!

With a deep breath in and shoulders back, I sucked in my gut and allowed her to take what would likely be the last images of my real breasts—my *real* breasts, real. This was me. Someone who hardly wore makeup, not because I didn't need it but because I grew up as more of a tomboy. I worked in a gym, where most times you could find me in workout clothes and a baseball cap. That wasn't to say I was careless about my appearance, but it was what I felt beautiful in, confident in. I just never pictured implants for myself. I certainly knew plenty of women who had them, and they looked gorgeous, but it was never on my radar.

As the nurse's camera clicked away, I began to picture my chest, flattened, with three scars. Two would be from the mastectomy and one from the lumpectomy. *Am I ready for this?* I quietly thought to myself. Something of that magnitude, cutting off a piece of my body? A part of my body that nurtured my children. A piece of myself that sensually connected me with my husband...gone. It would be different; how could it not be?

After the nurse was through taking the pictures she needed, the doctor came in briefly to see if I had any questions for him, which I did not; the nurse pretty much had covered everything. I left my appointment and headed back to work. By now, word had gotten around that I would be out for a significant amount of time. My group activities classes needed to be subbed out for several months, and I would also have to pull back from coaching my CORE Method, which was weighing on me heavily. People began to talk, to speculate even more. Most of them wanted to help, and I am sure finding the right words was an impossible expectation to have at such a sensitive time. But some things being said were just plain shitty. Likely said out of naivete, but they hurt just the same.

I started to hide in my office instead of being out on the gym floor. I figured out quick that if I dodged people, I wouldn't be left feeling so vulnerable and sensitive. Sensitive, numb, angry, tired... That was how I fumbled through my days, and now there were only fourteen until my mastectomy.

My feelings were all over the place, between facing the physical changes and riding the emotional roller coaster of many people trying to "help." Helpful statements that would have given me comfort during that time could have been, "You are brave. I think you are making the right decision." Or, "You are beautiful and not alone through any of this." Or, simply, "I am here for you."

Thank God for blessing me with family and friends who did find those comforting words. I needed to remind myself to lean more on them; they truly wanted to help simply because they loved me.

Since losing my mom, I swear she was doing her job as my guardian angel by placing the right people in my path throughout that horrific year.

In my life since childhood, I've had important friendships. Friends I met through having kids, through social circles, and through my workplace. God has had a beautiful way of placing what and who I needed in my life at the most perfect time, and His timing was never wrong. Perhaps some of the things I was experiencing since losing my mom could have been chalked up to pure coincidence, but I wanted to believe it was more.

In the final week before my surgery, reality started to sink in further. Maybe it was "normal" to be experiencing an enormous amount of dread; I didn't know. Although I remained confident in my decision, that didn't prevent all the emotions from continuing to rise to the surface.

When I found myself catching glimpses of myself naked in the mirror, I would pause. An image I once took for granted, I now relished in, as if I realized I needed to honor the final few days of my body. A body I knew so well, what it was capable of, and what it looked like. In just one week, it would be different.

Maybe that was what I was dreading, how different my body would be. Would I accept my new boobs and the scars across my chest, or would they bring on more of the feelings of depression and anxiety I had struggled with in the past? I was hyperaware of falling back down that rabbit hole.

My first experience with anxiety, followed by depression, was after I had my first child.

I remember lying in bed trying to get some sleep the first night we brought our beautiful baby girl home. Brian fell fast asleep, and Bailey was sleeping soundly in her newborn bassinet next to our bed. I lay there, staring at the ceiling, wide awake, when an enormous feeling of worry came over me. It wasn't about anything specific. I wasn't worried whether she was okay or anything like that. That was the thing: *It wasn't about anything in particular.* It was just a feeling of overwhelming uncertainty that I had never experienced until that night.

In the days that followed, those feelings became more intense. They would come in waves, and I couldn't explain why.

One day I brought Bailey to her pediatrician's office for a well visit. He asked me how I was doing, and spontaneously I burst into tears.

"If she would only sleep more than two hours, I think I would be okay!" I cried to him.

He replied, "Have you spoken with your own doctor about how you are feeling? You may be experiencing postpartum depression. It's really pretty common." He explained to me that Bailey had acid reflux, which was why she was not sleeping much. Needless to say, after we figured out her stomach problems and my hormonal ones, in time we both got better.

I didn't experience any postpartum depression after I had Collin. I attribute that to being better prepared for what to expect. Knowing that I could be susceptible to those awful feelings again, I made sure I got back to some of the things I loved to do right away. Things like going for a hike, a walk, or spending time with my girlfriends. When I became a mother for the first time, I think I believed that by stepping into that role, I had to give up who I was before. That, I learned, was far from the case. The woman I was before motherhood wasn't gone forever; in fact, that person would help to shape our family. Although things in my life would be prioritized differently, I slowly regained myself.

Preparing for how I would cope with things after the surgery reminded me of how I had prepared to avoid postpartum depression a second time around.

Molly advised me to have a few good books on hand, movies, and plenty of pillows to prop myself up, because it would be a long time before I would be allowed to sleep flat on my back. She also suggested getting my underarm hair waxed, because it would be a while before I could reach on my own to shave! That never had occurred to me, so for the weeks leading up to my surgery date, I grew out my underarm hair long enough to have it waxed. I also scheduled an appointment to have my hair done. I wanted to go into surgery feeling and looking my best. This was a surgery that was sure to test my self-confidence, and a little highlighting never hurt anyone, so why the hell not?

Along with my self-care, I took the time to prepare and freeze a few meals that Brian could easily pull out to heat and serve during my recovery time, when I wasn't feeling well enough to cook.

As much as I tried to preoccupy my brain in the days before my surgery, emotions kept rising up. Prepping food for the meals I wanted to freeze, it hit me again. I was scared and I missed my mom. I felt my emotions coming to the top like water about to boil in the pot on my stovetop.

As I was meal prepping, Collin was in the living room doing homework. I quickly shut down the gas and dashed to my bedroom closet to protect my son from hearing my sobs. Nothing stopped the tears that followed from the tidal wave of emotions that almost knocked me to the ground.

I began to beg for my mom. A forty-year-old woman, begging for her mommy. A mother she needed, deeply.

If only she were here, she would hold me now, I said to myself. I could picture in my mind coming home from the hospital to her cooking those meals, not me. We would watch movies in bed. She would rub my feet and paint my nails. That was the kind of mother she truly was, not the addict who took over her soul. Her true soul was selfless. The one who rubbed my head for hours when I was a child because I suffered from migraines. Literally for hours until I fell asleep to find the only relief from such horrible pain. She would probably laugh her ass off at the rash that was likely to happen the next day when I waxed off the underarm hair, followed by, "Why the hell would you do such a thing to yourself?"

Most of all, she would just be present to make me feel safe when I felt so scared.

The stark reality was that she was not there, and I didn't know how to make the pain go away myself. The pain of the surgery and its aftermath. The pain of losing my mom. The pain of not knowing if she was okay. It continued to hit me in waves that I still had not learned to ride out gracefully. I was barely staying afloat on this wave, with my hand over my mouth to muffle the pathetic sounds coming from deep within my body. I whimpered aloud at yet another attempt to reach my mother, who was no longer a part of this world.

"I miss you, Mom; I want you here with me. You should be here with me. God damn it! I shouldn't have to go through this without you. Why??? Why the hell is this happening? I need you, please, please, please..."

Just then I heard a sweet voice from the living room..." Mommy, I'm done with my homework."

I paused to steady my voice before answering. "Okay...be right there." I wiped my face, took a few deep breaths, and joined my son.

The days before my surgery were one giant, emotional roller coaster ride. After the cryfest for my mommy, I decided to call Kimberly to vent. She had told me to lean on her, and I was going to.

"Valerie, did you ever check out the Facebook page I told you about? Stupid Dumb Breast Cancer?"

Stupid Dumb Breast Cancer is a resource page founded by a woman named Ann Marie who was from my hometown of Syracuse. She was diagnosed with breast cancer in 2012 and decided to help others by creating a page where people battling it could go for information, ask questions, or just gain support. At first when Kimberly told me to check it out, I didn't think this page would apply to me because I didn't have cancer.

"Valerie," she insisted, "I am telling you, this woman is amazing! I think you'll find you have a lot in common with her, and I have to believe what you are feeling is what a lot of other women on that page are feeling too. Please check it out."

So, I did.

When I clicked on Ann Marie's Stupid Dumb Breast Cancer page, I found a community of women warriors—mostly breast cancer survivors, but also survivors of other cancers and their caregivers. Women who were just diagnosed as well as longtime survivors, and also women taking their first steps toward making a decision like mine, to go with a preventive measure. It was a page where you could ask anything, without judgment, and you would receive experience- and knowledge-based information and also love and support. Women spoke openly and candidly about their diagnosis, treatment plans, and side effects. Everything, down to what sort of bras, camisoles, scar creams, and other items worked best. There was even a checklist of what you would need in the hospital and at home when undergoing a mastectomy.

I also found photos. I had seen photos before, and Molly had shared her journey with me, but I had never seen the whole process, from premastectomy to post-.

Ann Marie documented her entire journey, taking photos along the way. She shared some of those images on the Facebook page. I knew the photos existed before I visited the page; Kimberly told me about them. She thought it would help calm some of my fears about what a mastectomy would look like and how the process would be for me because Ann Marie was a woman around my age and relatable.

I skimmed through her page, then headed right to her photo section. There were so many pictures. At first, I saw the pictures of events she'd organized to raise money for various cancer organizations, as well as the photos of her family and friends and inspirational quotes. Then I came across the photos I was curious to see: the ones of her mastectomy and reconstruction. When I clicked on the first, my immediate reaction was how beautiful and brave this woman was to share her images in this way. The photo was of Ann Marie, lying down, with both breasts exposed. It showed her scars, the still in her left arm, as well as a beautiful tattoo of a butterfly above her right breast. The photo caption read, "This is the reality of cancer. Cancer has offended my body, why does this offend someone else?" I could tell right away that this woman was fierce, a force to be reckoned with. She'd opened herself up to a wealth of criticism by posting photos like these. I clicked on more photos and read some of the older comments. I learned that she'd fought to keep the images up—there was constant protest about them. Some viewed them as offensive, even pornographic. When I read that, it infuriated me. Our society has a messed-up perspective about what is offensive, and the pictures Ann Marie shared were certainly not pornographic. The only thing offensive to me was the ignorance of people who judged something they knew nothing about. If they didn't agree with what she was sharing, why were they on her page?

Ann Marie seemed to be willing to take on all the negativity, to tell the haters to "poof, be gone," as she put it, "you have no power here." Her mission was to help women like me.

After logging off her page, I did feel better. It helped immensely to read a little more about how this surgery was for some. To see her photos and her vulnerability made me feel like I wouldn't be as alone as I thought. There was an entire community of other women I could reach out to, right at my fingertips.

Visiting her page gave me an idea: Maybe I should document my process too. It might be a good thing to do in case another woman I knew had to go through a mastectomy too. At the very least I could make an album of my journey to share, if need be, and I knew just the person to entrust it to.

My friend Trish, who lived in our town, was a very accomplished photographer. She had covered everything from events for our local newspaper to ballet recitals and headshots. Surely photographing my breasts—and the lack of them at some point—would be within her repertoire.

It started with a text: "Hey Trish, I have an idea, call me when you have a sec."

Without hesitation, Trish agreed to document my journey, starting with some "before" pictures that were much less clinical than the ones taken by the nurse at my plastic surgeon's office. The "before" images she took in my home just days prior to the surgery, captured my chest before the changes that were to come.

When Trish arrived she scoped out a few rooms and decided to take the photos in the living room, in front of our picture window, where natural light poured in. Wearing only a Bohemian-style, flowing skirt, I stood in front of the window and posed. I am not at all comfortable in front of the camera and couldn't help but wonder if any of my neighbors could see my tits through the window and wondered what the hell was going on.

Trish clicked away, and together we experimented with different poses so she would have many images to choose from. Later that day, she sent me a picture for a sneak peek. There was my profile with my right arm over my head. I observed the smooth lines of my body, starting from my arm reaching over my head, around my breast, down my ribs to my hips…natural, naked me. I stared at that picture and thought of how I would be altering that profile. The next time I raised my arm up that way, would you see the implant from the side? How about the scars and my fake tattooed nipples, if I choose to get them? It would *all* be different. Those thoughts and so many others played over and over in my mind in the days before my surgery, and that familiar feeling of dread consumed me again.

I reasoned with myself that no matter what my thoughts and feelings were, they were mine. It was up to me to decide how I was going to handle all this. No, my mother was not here, yet I had wonderful friends, a supportive husband, a strong and protective sister, and other family to support me and vent to when I needed to. But it was ultimately all up to me to get to the other side of this. The bad days would be sure to come during recovery, and when they did, it would be up to me to turn them around.

There was one last appointment before surgery day, and that was to see my plastic surgeon once again so he could mark up the areas where the incisions would be. Trish accompanied me to start documenting the process.

As soon as we walked into the examining room, we both thought the same thing and said aloud, "The lighting in here is perfect!" Trish took a place in the corner, out of the way, to quietly capture more images to document as much as she could. My doctor began marking the areas where my breast surgeon would do "her job," and I noticed he gave her two options with my left breast: to include the scar from my lumpectomy or not. Of course I hoped she would not have to include it, because it seemed it would make for a much larger scar, and I shared my opinion with him. He quickly reminded me that my breast surgeon would do whatever was right for my health and he would do his job afterward. Health first…cosmetics were *not* the priority. Reality check!

After he was finished making all his markings, he placed clear tape over the areas and asked me not to get it excessively wet, meaning no long showers and no more exercise before surgery. What? I still had four more days to go! I was hoping to get in a Zumba class with Bailey later that day, and maybe a run over the weekend… Ugh. I guess that was off the table.

With just the weekend left before surgery day, I chose to clean my house like it had never shone before! It gave me something to do so my nerves couldn't get the best of me.

A few families who Brian and I had grown very close to in the last few years wanted to get together for dinner that weekend before

I was laid up. Our kids all knew one another and were included, so that was nice.

Pepe and Cheryl Caridad were like family to us, and they agreed to host the dinner for all our friends, a generous sentiment to wish me luck. We had the kids eat first so they could head off to play, allowing the adults to settle into the dining room for the lovely meal laid out there. Before we began to eat, one of the husbands interrupted for a toast—"To Valerie, one of the bravest women I know"—he stated simply, which blew me away for two reasons: that a statement like that came from one of the guys at the table and that anyone even felt that way. I certainly wasn't feeling brave…far from it. I was still feeling scared, stressed, sad, ridden with anxiety, and somewhat still alone…far from brave. I wondered if anyone at that table realized that. Probably not; I usually did a pretty good job of putting up a strong front. After all, I'd learned that from the best: my mom. They were all such caring, empathetic people, and I knew if I needed any one of them at any time, they would be there, part of the tribe I kept very close to me during that time.

But that evening I refused to get emotional, and I could feel myself doing just that. I fell short of saying anything other than a soft, "Thank you all."

Thankfully the somber tone was interrupted when somebody clanked another's glass and Pepe yelled, "Crap, now you've started it! A whole mammajamma!" "Mammajamma" was another word for a situation, an issue, a dilemma, an obstacle. Well…you get the picture.

It was a tradition among our friends that whenever you gave a toast, you could either raise your glass and take a sip or raise your glass and tap someone else's. But if you tapped someone's glass, everyone must follow suit, which takes a little more time when all you want to do is eat! In this case, it was the perfect thing to do to lighten the mood, a little mammajamma, if you will, so I wasn't reduced to tears.

On my final day of work before I took time off to recover, I coached a five thirty morning class called the Bad Ass Breakfast Club. Those members were also known as my peeps.

I began coaching everyone through a strength training and did my best to do so without getting my markings wet with perspiration. After class I finished up some loose ends in the office and submitted payroll. Then I hugged my clients and team members and headed out for the day. My plan was to return to work in two weeks—well, to return to my desk job anyway.

The kids would be home soon, and I was really looking forward to spending some time with them. Bailey had a late night at dance, taking a jazz class she loved, and Collin and I decided to wait for her, snuggled up in my bed, reading. He loved cozying up in mommy and daddy's bed. In fact, the whole family often somehow found their way to our bed at day's end, dog included! It was an adjustable bed that could be raised for reading and soon would be perfect for me to sleep in, on my back, on an incline. It was very cozy, fuzzy blankets and all. I imagine that was why everyone convened in our bedroom at night before heading off to their own.

With Collin, I tried to focus on things we could do together when I got home from the hospital, and reading was one of them. He and I were the bookworms in our household. I made a promise to him that when Mommy came home from the hospital, we would have plenty of time to read together. That gave him something to look forward to. He still was unaware of the details of my surgery, and at eight years old, he didn't need to know them. I tried to answer the questions he had along the way without offering any information he hadn't asked for.

When Bailey arrived home just before nine o'clock, it was already time for bed. Selfishly, I wanted to squeeze them tight and let them both sleep with me that night, but I thought that would reveal that I was worried. Instead, I tucked them in their own beds and said the special prayer we'd recited together their whole lives: "In the name of Jesus, Mary, and Joseph, may your guardian angels watch over and protect you all night long and all day long. Amen." Prayers said, I kissed each of them good night, lingering a little longer with my hugs than I usually did.

The next morning, I awoke to the alarm set for five thirty, plenty of time to get ready for my seven thirty arrival time at the hospital. Sticking with the plan of trying to keep things as normal as possible for the kids, I began making them breakfast, which was killing me because I couldn't have anything to eat or drink. The sweet and savory scents of their waffles as I heated them, and their oranges as I peeled them, were pure torture, not to be outdone by the smell of the fresh-brewed coffee Brian was waving in front of my face.

After a quick bite for Bailey and Collin, it was time for Bailey to head to the bus stop and for me to drop Collin off at our neighbor's house so she could give him a ride to school.

"I love you and I will see you both tomorrow, okay?" I said reassuringly, though neither of them showed any signs that they needed any comforting from me at all. Carefree, they each shouted back, "'Bye, Mom!" And off they went.

I arrived promptly for my surgery. There were so many people in the waiting room, which made my mind race with curiosity, wondering what brought them to the hospital. Like the young teenage girl, laughing with her mom as they sat and waited. *I bet she is in here because of a sports injury.* I hoped it was nothing more, secretly jealous that she was sitting with her mom, while mine was gone. There was an elderly man sitting a few seats down from me, hacking away. Maybe he was here for a lung transplant. Sure sounded like he could use a new pair!

Ding, my phone chimed. I looked down to find a funny selfie from my sister, and I decided to return the sentiment. The elderly man caught a glimpse of me making a ridiculous face at my phone and rolled his eyes, followed by more hacking.

I didn't care—I snapped a quick "duck face" selfie and texted it to Monica.

"Hey, why don't we have any of these subscriptions at home?" Brian asked me while he thumbed through a magazine.

"I don't know. Seriously, Brian, you want me to order you a gardening magazine?" I was certain he was just trying to break the silence in the waiting room.

We only waited fifteen minutes for my name to be called.

"Mrs. Walsh, we are ready for you. Please follow me. Your husband may come with you while we begin your prep. What is your full name and birthdate?"

"Valerie Walsh, November 16, 1973."

We followed her into a small examining room. "Okay, Valerie, I am going to ask you to get into this paper gown and use the restroom to leave a urine sample for me."

There was a small bathroom across the way from the room Brian and I were in. I headed to the restroom to change into my paper gown and left my urine sample as instructed. When I went back into the examining room, the nurse set me up in a very comfortable recliner and attached a hose to an opening in my paper gown.

"This will blow warm air inside your gown. Here is the remote so you can control the temperature," the nurse explained.

What an amazing invention. People should have these in their homes to use while they kick back and watch TV! I turned up the remote for maximum heat; it was February and very cold the morning of my mastectomy.

A short time later a surgical nurse came in to take my vitals and prep the IV. I think this was the worst part for me. I hated getting an IV put in my arm. Shots never bothered me much, but IVs? No, thank you! Fortunately, it went in smoothly.

Next, the anesthesiologist entered the room and asked me about any medications I was taking, if I had allergies, and if I had any last-minute questions.

"No questions, just be sure you keep me comfortable and wake me up," I said to him.

He glanced up from his paperwork, his eyeglasses resting on the bridge of his nose, smiled, and said in a somewhat cocky way, "That's our specialty. I will see you in the operating room, Valerie." He turned to Brian and promised to take good care of me.

Finally, my breast surgeon came in to briefly discuss the entire procedure once again, then asked me, "Which side are we operating on?"

"The left side," I replied, and she smiled. Trick question…she got me. Before heading to the operating room (where I would see her again), she marked both my breasts with smiley faces because we were going to have a good day. Maybe she wasn't so bad after all.

This was it, go time, and also time for me to say goodbye to Brian.

"I love you; you're going to be just fine," he assured me as he had been doing all these months in overtime, since last May, when I buried my mom. With each doctor's appointment, with all the uncertainty, anger, and sadness, he was there to pull me in. This time he pulled me in closer and held me until my name was called once more.

The surgical nurse led me down the dramatically bright hallway and into the operating room.

The room was filled with many people—some I recognized, others I did not. Off in the corner, I noticed my surgeon, writing on a clipboard, concentrating so intently on her work that she didn't even look up when I entered the room.

A few nurses assisted me up on to the operating table and placed my arms straight out, like the letter t, just as they had when

I had my lumpectomy two months before. The room felt so cold, perhaps done purposefully so the surgical team remained alert for such a long procedure; they informed me this would be about an eight-hour operation.

In the background, music was playing. Pop music, the same kind I exercised to. I put my head back, and the anesthesiologist placed a mask over my mouth and told me to count back from ten. It was up to me now, ten…nine…eight—

TEN

Physical Healing

"Even the moon passes through phases to return to full."

~SONIA MOTWANI

Phase 1: February 11, 2014

"Mrs. Walsh...Mrs. Walsh, everything went really well, and we are taking you back to recovery now," I heard a voice say faintly in the background. I felt like I was waking up from a nap, and I would've liked to have kept on sleeping, so I wanted to tell whomever it was to please go away. "We are going to bring you some ice chips in a bit and let your husband know you did just great." Oh, it was coming back to me now...

I knew where I was.

With my eyes halfway open, I panned around the room in a daze. I could see some people sleeping, some awake, a few moaning in pain. Lucky for me, I was not in any pain, just tired and groggy. A few moments later a gentleman, perhaps a few years older than me, was wheeled into the room and his gurney was placed just a few feet away from mine. The nurses began to explain to him that the doctor was not able to perform his hip replacement surgery because he had a cut on the bottom of his foot that was infected.

It wasn't until he was completely under anesthesia and they were ready to start his operation that they made the discovery by taking off his socks on the operating table.

As they continued to explain their reasons for postponing his procedure, he began to cry. "You don't understand," he tried telling the nurses, "I am a builder, self-employed. I delayed jobs to have this done today! I have guys counting on me for work and this messes with my entire schedule!"

I was sure the anesthesia played a part in his emotions, but I also assumed he must have prepared for weeks, maybe even months, to have his surgery done now. Married to someone self-employed myself, I felt terrible for this man, but at the same time I felt a sense of relief for myself. My surgery was done and, from what I'd been told, a success.

The hospital was extremely busy. I waited for hours in that recovery room, anxious to see Brian and talk with my family. The nurses walked by occasionally, assuring me that they would let him in "soon."

It was a very bizarre atmosphere. A large room crammed full of beds that held people who were all half out of it. We said nothing to one another as we faded in and out of our slumber.

I knew my breast navigator, the one from the surgeon's office, had arranged for a private room for me that would allow Brian to spend the night. Finally, just before seven thirty that night, he walked into the recovery room.

"Hey, how are you feeling?" he asked.

"Okay, just a little hungry."

One of the nurse's overheard our conversation and walked right over to hand me a menu.

"If you place your order quickly, I might be able to get it in before the kitchen closes. You too, Brian," she said to us both.

Brian never missed an opportunity to eat and hovered over my shoulders to check out the selections.

"Just pick something for me, but make sure they have choco-late pudding," I said, because I couldn't even hold the menu up or keep my eyes open any longer.

Shortly after Brian placed an order of grilled chicken with brown rice and a cup of chocolate pudding, I was wheeled up to my room. Just as promised, our dinner was waiting for us, along with a beautiful bouquet of flowers from my sister, which reminded me to ask Brian if he'd called her yet.

"Did you let her know everything is good? What did she say?" I asked him.

"Your sister and I have been texting all day; she knows," he quickly answered, then handed me my cell phone so I could text her. Her text back to me read, "Well look who is cancer free, you did it and I am so proud of you!" I smiled and let out a huge sigh of relief.

I did it. I took my physical health in my own hands and made a difficult choice to reduce my risk for breast cancer. I wanted so desperately to believe my mother had been right by my side to guide me, but in truth, I still couldn't feel her. I had yet to receive any signs, any indication that somehow, some way, she knew from whatever spiritual realm she was floating in, that this shitshow was going on, all without her.

While I wallowed in pain and a bit of sadness yet again, think-ing of facing my circumstances without my mom, I was quickly reminded that I was a mother too, and I needed to call my kids. I decided waiting a little longer would be a better idea, because I was still feeling the effects of the anesthesia and my throat was killing me from the breathing tube. Maybe after I got a little food in my stomach, I would feel better.

Eating the chicken was like chewing on a piece of rubber, and my mouth was very dry, as if I had never tried chewing before and it was a very awkward task. Every move I attempted to make felt like I was doing it through quicksand, in slow motion. I picked up the chocolate pudding and decided it was a nutritious enough option for me after not eating all day.

My aunt Donna was staying with the kids at our house during my hospital stay. When I called the house, she answered the phone, and I could hear both of the kids whispering in the background as she was catching me up on the day's events.

"Is that my mom?" Bailey asked. "How is she? Can I talk to her first?"

Collin was so excited to have Aunt Donna there for an over-night, he seemed less concerned about me than his big sister. As Bailey caught me up on her day, I could hear Collin in the back-ground, negotiating his bedtime and explaining where everything in the house was. I decided to let the false information about their normal bedtime slide; it was a "special occasion," having their great-aunt Donna there. After I reassured them both that I would be home later the next day, we ended our conversation with our evening prayer and said our good nights.

I was placed on a pain pump to keep me comfortable. My hos-pital care was impeccable. Each nurse and orderly who attended to me was right on top of everything—a little bit too much at times, making it hard for me to get any decent sleep.

Just as I tried to doze off again, it hit me…I had to pee. Crap, this meant getting up for the first time. Ugh.

"What can I do?" Brian asked.

"Get the nurse; they told me to let them know when I have to use the bathroom."

Brian went out into the hallway and returned with a very young and very handsome male nurse. "Hi, Valerie, my name is Grant."

Grant? Seriously, I could not have picked a better name to match his adorable nature.

"Let's get you up, slowly…okay?" he instructed me. Then, he began to adjust my bed to a more comfortable position so I could get out of it on my own. "Valerie, they are going to want to see that you can do this part by yourself before you can go home. You have to be able to get yourself up without assistance," Grant explained to me. "It is one of the tests you have to pass."

That was enough motivation for me to try to do it without his help. Slowly, I began to lift up my torso without relying on my arms, using my core muscles instead. I wiggled my bum down far enough to allow myself to swing both of my legs over the bed, and slowly, very slowly, I stood up—only halfway. "Oh...oh...oh...wait, wait...that hurts," I whined, and dizziness set in.

"What is it, is something wrong? What can I do?" Brian asked with concern.

"It's okay, she's okay, this is the worst part, getting up and down. It will get better for her in time," Grant promised both of us. It was then that I realized I was not his first breast surgery patient and he had done this many times before.

Once I stood up on my own, I began the slow, methodical walk toward the bathroom, breathing through the pain that was setting in with each tiny step. What happened next made me very thankful for all the squats I had ever done in my life and the countless number of times I'd had to hover to pee in public restrooms.

Sweet baby Jesus, I did it...my first solo pee postsurgery. It was the little things—well, in that case, big. That was the biggest pee I'd taken in a long time!

Three in the morning and I still couldn't sleep. Instead, my ears stayed tuned in to this annoying woman right outside my room. Seems her mother was being admitted because she had taken a hard fall, and the way it sounded, she would need surgery in the morning.

I could sense the woman growing more and more impatient at each question the nurse was throwing at her. "Is this all really necessary? I mean, you should have all this information for my mother; we have been in here enough! Why the hell do you need all this information right now? I'm exhausted and I'd like to get my mother settled into a room so I can go home and sleep!" the woman blurted out.

She continued to unleash a list of the inconveniences, or "shit," as she so graciously put it, she had been through with her mother over the last few months. Even from my bed, it was obvious she'd had it. She was overwhelmed and at her breaking point. The woman wanted to be sure anyone who was within earshot knew what she was feeling, including me, even if I was trying to sleep.

As she continued her rant, I became angrier with her. So much so, I wanted to scream back at her, "What the hell is wrong with you? That is your mother you're talking about, and she needs your help! You should feel blessed that you still have her with you, you foolish, selfish woman!" Oh, how I would have loved to have mustered up the strength to have gotten out of my bed, grab her by the shoulders, and shaken some sense into her.

Instead, I minded my own business. Stress can bring out the worst in any of us. I trusted that perhaps I was overhearing a brief weak moment from this woman.

Now I was wide awake and reminded of my own weak moments with my mother. There were many, and I still deeply regretted each and every one of them. So many times, I had felt put out, inconvenienced, not equipped with enough life experience to handle her gracefully. What I wouldn't give to be out in that hallway, helping my own mother. I would do it all differently if given a second chance. I would say everything—every single thought, the good, the bad, and the ugly—I had stored in my brain over the course of the nine months since her death. But I couldn't. So, I stared up at the ceiling, praying quietly in my head as I had countless times before. *Mom, can you hear me? If you can, would you please show me a sign? Anything—flicker the light, let me dream of you when I fall asleep—something, please?*

I'd had only one vague dream of my mother since her death. Barely a glimpse, and not one single sign—although I had convinced myself that her angel stone may have been one—to reassure me that she finally had found peace. The thought of her not resting peacefully fucked with both my mind and my spirit. Maybe she wasn't coming to me because she was angry with me? Maybe she was stuck in some in-between state and learning more lessons? Or maybe she simply wasn't ready, and maybe…neither was I.

I had already asked God for forgiveness. I could only continue to quietly pray that my mother knew how I felt as well. Someday the woman in the hallway would likely wish the same, bear the same regrets that she hadn't been more compassionate and patient with her mother.

Six in the morning and I still hadn't slept. I pressed the Call button for the nurse. "Yes, Mrs. Walsh?" someone responded.

"I have to pee," I said, feeling somewhat embarrassed to have to ask for help again.

In walked my wonderful nurse, Grant, who had been helping me all night. He came over to my bed and got right to making all the adjustments needed so I could get up as comfortably as possible.

With all the shifting and moving about, Brian woke up. "Is everything okay?" he asked, half asleep.

"Yes, I just have to pee…again," I whispered to him, "but don't worry, *Grant* has me," I teased.

As I cautiously rose to my feet, Grant started to help me with my gown, allowing for some discretion in the entire process. "I really don't care if my ass is hanging out at this point. I have had two kids, so let's just get that out of the way!" He and Brian laughed at my response as I slowly shuffled my way to the bathroom. When I finished, I figured as long as I was up, I might as well try to walk a few laps around the hallway. Grant permitted this, and Brian joined me. We walked three times around the areas they allowed us to use for "laps." This would be my first challenge to myself: Each time I needed to get up to use the bathroom I would walk, adding a lap.

When we returned from our walk, it was time for Brian to leave for work. Being a business owner presented a long list of challenges, like not being able to take too much time off. The reality was when Brian wasn't working, our household did not bring in any money. Yes, I worked, and my job did help with some of the expenses, but Brian was our primary breadwinner, and without his income our financial burdens would become even greater than they already were.

Before he headed out for the day I asked him to run to the café downstairs and please get me a coffee. I was dying for a hot cup of coffee; my throat was still sore from the tube, plus maybe it would help me poop, which was apparently another goal they set for me before I would be allowed to leave the hospital.

While Brian was out on my coffee run, a group of young interns, about six of them, entered my room, along with a doctor I had never seen before.

"Good morning," the doctor said as she entered my room, hardly looking up from her clipboard. She continued on, without introducing herself or the strangers who were all crammed into my room. She began to discuss my case as if I were not even present. "Here we have a forty-year-old female who has just undergone a prophylactic bilateral mastectomy."

There was that word again, "prophylactic." Eww. She went on to describe my case in full detail to the interns, who were standing quietly holding their clipboards, all staring directly at me. I felt like a zoo animal on display.

There was a brief moment when the doctor showed a little compassion by asking, "How are you feeling this morning, Mrs. Walsh?"

"Okay."

I don't know if it was my answer or her utter disregard for the fact that I was a woman who had just had her breasts cut off, but what happened next was crushing: Without asking permission, she lowered the front of my gown and began lifting off my dressing to show the interns my surgery and what "it"—her words, not mine—looked like.

I said nothing at first. I couldn't seem to find the words. Instead, I started to cry. The doctor immediately stopped what she was doing and pulled my gown back up. "What's wrong? Are you okay? Are you experiencing any pain?" she asked, completely clueless at what she had just done.

Through my tears I answered, "It's just too much. *I haven't even seen myself,* I'm not ready for this audience to see me. I'm sorry, I am just really emotional."

The room fell silent. Embarrassment sank in. I began feeling bad for making *them* feel bad. I have no idea why the fuck I felt that way. I knew I shouldn't have cared about their feelings, but I was fragile, and I did. I continued to apologize for my reaction. "It's okay...it's okay, I am just really emotional, it's probably all the medicine."

The young interns didn't know which way to look or what to say, so they just walked out, leaving only the doctor behind. She wished me luck with my recovery and promptly left my room. I guess her years of medical school failed to teach her to have a heart, the idiot. Hopefully the interns who made rounds with her that morning took with them a lesson in compassion and not just clinical findings.

Brian returned with my coffee to find me upset. He immediately noticed and asked, "What happened, are you in pain?"

"No, some asshole doctor just came into my room with a bunch of interns. It sucked, the whole thing. She didn't even ask if it would be okay to show my chest, she just did it!" I sobbed in his arms, the first tears to my husband since my breasts were cut off. Not from any physical pain, but from shame.

Brian was furious. "What the fuck? Want me to say something, make a complaint?"

"No, leave it alone, I just want to get some rest." I knew he felt bad that this had happened while he'd stepped out to get my coffee. If he had been there, it would not have happened. There would have been no way he would have let a group of strangers in to see me put on display. It wasn't his fault; I'd asked him to go get my coffee. I didn't want him to file a complaint, I just wanted to forget about the whole incident. Brian was a wonderful advocate for me during my hospital stay. Maybe it was a good thing he went for that coffee run. Otherwise that doctor may have found herself as a patient in the hospital, removing a clipboard from up her ass!

One thing was for sure—that was *not* how I'd pictured my first reveal.

The plan for the day was to send Brian back to the house to check in with my aunt Donna, but now he was hesitating about leaving.

"I'm fine now. I just needed to calm down," I promised him.

"Okay. But if you get released before dinner, what will we do?" Brian asked.

"Call Ashley. She said you could; she is off today. Seriously, she wants to help." Ashley was a family friend. Brian had gone to high school with her, and now our daughters were in high school together. She had offered her help to us before, saying she would be available if we needed her.

"Are you sure?" Brian checked, feeling guilty at making plans for someone other than himself to pick me up. Truly, it was no big deal. We were set to get over a foot of snow by the next day, so Brian might be stuck plowing, and life went on; he needed to work.

With my ride in place, Brian kissed my forehead and headed off for the day.

Within a few hours after he left, there was a changing of the guard of the overnight team of nurses and orderlies. Before heading out from his shift, Grant popped his head into my room to say, "You're going to do great, Valerie. Take good care of yourself, okay?"

"I will," I promised him. I was going to miss my guy Grant. The daytime nurse came into my room a few minutes later to introduce herself. She was no Grant, but she seemed pleasant enough, although when she started to adjust my bed and shift things around to the way she thought I would be more comfortable, I started to rethink my open mind about her. As well-meaning as her efforts were, they were for nothing. As soon as she left, I fixed everything right back to the way I'd had it, including the TV remote, which she had placed so far away I couldn't reach it. What the hell, where was Grant?

I just wanted to go home to my own bed, with my own bedside table, which I had already set up with special items to help keep me comfortable: candle, books, my medicines laid out and organized, my ChapStick, soft tissues, and lavender hand cream. Plus there was one more thing I'd add when I got home...a back scratcher! My pain medications made me itch terribly, and not being able to reach those spots was so frustrating.

The Christmas before, Collin used his own money and bought me a back scratcher at his holiday school store. He was so cute when he gave it to me. Little did he know that his present would come in handy so soon! I would also have to tell Ann Marie to add a back scratcher to the list of items to pack for the hospital on her Stupid Dumb Breast Cancer Facebook page—it was a must-have.

Just as I started to finally nod off, the nurse returned, this time not to make any annoying adjustments to my setup, but rather with good news. "Well, Mrs. Walsh, it looks like they are going to try to release you sometime after lunch today. Your breast navigator will stop by to go over the at-home care instructions and to be sure you are comfortable with everything."

I loved that the breast navigator would check on me. She was the person I went to with most of my questions. A kind, compassionate, and very positive woman, it was no surprise she held that position.

Well, it looked as if I wasn't going to get much sleep, so I decided to put in my lunch order. The hospital had it set up more like room service—I was able to select from the menu provided and phone in my order. I decided on an egg salad sandwich on toasted gluten-free bread, a side of mashed sweet potatoes, and two cups of cranberry juice. An eclectic selection, but that was what was calling out to me.

However, when my food arrived, the only thing I could manage to get down was the bowl of mashed sweet potatoes and the two cups of cranberry juice. The egg salad didn't appeal to me in the same way it had when I ordered it—in fact, it made me nauseous—so I quickly pushed it aside.

As promised, my breast navigator arrived just as I was finishing my lunch. Ashley came in as well, ready to give me a ride home.

"Oh, Valerie, you look like you are doing so well. I knew you would!" the navigator proudly said to me. She was my biggest cheerleader, always supporting me since the very beginning of all this. With her, she brought a bag full of things I would need at home. All the dressings for around both drainage sites; a log to keep track, three times a day, of how much fluid I was dispensing; and a pretty camisole to wear as well.

She took the camisole out of the bag and said, "Okay, Valerie, we are going to get you out of that gown now and into this. I want you to go into the bathroom and see yourself. We like you to do this when you are still in the hospital, so you know what to expect and what is normal. I will be right outside the door if you need me, just call."

I didn't bother telling her I had had a quick glance at my chest earlier, when the interns came in. I didn't feel like rehashing the story.

Until then, my dressings had not been taken off fully, so I hadn't been able to see myself naked, without my breasts. The navigator carefully began the delicate task of removing the dressing as I sat at the edge of my bed. "Are you doing okay?" she asked with compassion in her voice.

"Yes...I am ready," I said and slowly walked into the bathroom.

Standing in the hospital bathroom under the fluorescent lights, I looked at myself for the first time, completely naked, without breasts. To my surprise, I felt calm. In fact, I felt relief. It truly wasn't as bad as I had thought it was going to be. I continued to stand there, staring at myself in the mirror, thinking, *You did it. Everything is going to be okay...it's all going to be okay. Now it's time to go home to your family*. I gently dressed, although before putting on my camisole, I asked my girlfriend if she wanted to see.

"Yes, if you don't mind, I would." Ashley had worked for a plastic surgeon for many years and had seen a fair number of bilateral mastectomies, so I knew she would know what to expect and be a good judge of what she saw.

"Valerie, I swear, the surgical site looks good. Your doctor did a great job. You will heal beautifully."

It helped to hear that from her.

Once I was all dressed, I signed my release papers and Ashley helped pack my bags so we could head out.

My breast navigator and I waited in the hospital lobby as Ashley got her car. "I want you to know you both have given me peace of mind; I really mean that. Thank you," I told her and asked that she pass the message on to my breast surgeon. She shared that she was so happy that I was able to make the right decision for myself and wished me well.

As we continued to wait for Ashley to arrive with the car, I pulled out my phone to share pictures of my kids.

"They're beautiful, how old?"

"Collin is eight and Bailey just turned fourteen this past weekend."

Moments later, Ashley's car pulled to the front of the building, and I was wheeled out into the chilly February air, ready to head home.

My homecoming was anything but smooth. The kids weren't home yet, and Brian was preoccupied with the impending snowstorm. He was there to greet me; however, I could see right away how anxious he was to get back on the road. Snow was already beginning to pile up, and he needed to keep plowing. Life doesn't stop, even in times like this. In fact, it continued with the same force as the snowstorm that was about to hit us.

Before going back to work, Brian ran over to Ashley's car to help bring me inside and get me settled. "Thank you for everything, Ash…we really appreciate it," Brian said as he carefully placed his arm out for me to hold on to and we walked inside.

Just as we shut the door to the house, we heard a big *bam*. Ashley had backed into a tree and completely smashed her entire rear windshield. Brian ran outside as I watched in disbelief. *You've got to be fucking kidding me with this*, I thought to myself.

No good deed goes unpunished, but luckily for us, Ashley was one cool chick. She got out of her car, laughed at the stupidity of it all, and said, "No worries, guys. Seriously, it's no big deal. That's what we have insurance for." She proceeded to drive home with snow falling through her now blown-out window.

Phase 2

My father-in-law, Pat, came to stay with me for a few days during the first part of my recovery. He was retired now, and when he heard that I would need someone with me, he jumped at the opportunity to help. As far as male nurses went, he was no Grant, but I was very happy to have him at home with me.

When Pat showed up with a bottle of Southern Comfort in his hand, I teased him, saying, "Good, I see you've brought your own medicine as well!"

"Sweetie, how are you feeling?"

"Doing okay, just tired. I can't stay on my feet long; I still feel so weak," I said to him.

"Well, go back to bed, and let me know if you need anything. I mean it; that's what I am here for," he assured me, and I headed back to my room to rest.

I tried to be a reasonable patient, with the occasional request for something. Most of the day I was laid up in my bed, dozing in and out of sleep. Most times all I needed were small adjustments of my pillows and something to drink, but I felt guilty all the same to keep asking for help. Getting comfortable was a constant annoyance, making sleep nearly impossible.

Each day I did what I was told: took my medicine on time, stayed hydrated, used my breathing device to help dissipate the anesthesia from my lungs, and recorded my drainage. I would see my plastic surgeon for a follow-up three days out from my surgery.

When the time came to go to his office, Trish drove me, as she continued to document my process along the way. When she arrived to pick me up, she noticed right away I wasn't feeling well. "What's wrong? Are you still in pain?" she asked.

"My head is *killing* me. I haven't taken anything for it yet—I can't remember if I am allowed to take aspirin or ibuprofen. It hurts more than my chest; I feel like I'm getting a migraine." My entire life I had been susceptible to migraines. I was hoping this headache wouldn't turn into one. However, the twenty-minute ride to the doctor's office, with my eyes barely open, quickly turned my headache into a full-blown migraine, and now I was starting to feel nauseous.

When I arrived, I immediately asked the nurse for something for my head, and she quickly returned with two aspirin. I closed my eyes and waited for the doctor to come in to check my surgical sites and drains.

"Looking good, Valerie. You are healing very well. Next appointment you will be about seven days out. We will look to see if your drains can come out then. Sound like a plan?"

"Yes, sounds good to me," I answered. I was anxious to get the drains out as soon as possible. They were a nuisance and, at times, very achy.

Trish was able to take a few more photos before she drove me home to allow me to get right back into bed. My migraine left me completely wiped out. The best medicine was to sleep it off.

The next morning I woke up with the same dull headache I'd started out with the day before, so I popped a couple of aspirin to keep it from progressing. It occurred to me that my pain medication may be triggering my migraines, so I decided to start weaning myself off them. Suffering a migraine, to me, was far worse than the surgical pain; they can be debilitating.

My father-in-law was a tremendous help during the few days he stayed with me, and I was going to miss having him around. Just knowing he was in the next room if I needed him was a great comfort.

Just when I thought I would have to gear up to take care of myself, Kimberly called. "Hey, you! How are you?" she asked with concern in her voice.

"Pretty good. I wish I could sleep better. Pat was here for a few days, but he headed out this morning."

"Well, guess what?" Kimberly said, leaving me in suspense for a moment…"My kids have this week off for winter break and Eric is working from home, so I am coming to visit you!"

My best friend came all the way from Syracuse to Connecticut to take care of me. As far as friendships went, this one remained one I could always count on. We shared the most intimate of information with each other, and now she would see me through a very trying time.

"I'm going to start out first thing in the morning," she informed me. "So, get some sleep tonight, and tomorrow…girl time begins!"

Kimberly texted me at around nine the next morning to let me know she was on the road, putting her in Connecticut at around one thirty in the afternoon. Next to my sis, she was probably the only woman I would want with me at a time like this.

When I spoke with Kimberly on the phone the night before, she'd told me that she looked forward to coming to just watch me sleep…kind of creepy, but I knew what she meant. She needed to see for herself that I was okay, and I had no problem with granting her wish, because that was all I seemed to be doing—trying to sleep. Sleeping on and off during the day wasn't a problem, but I still couldn't get comfortable enough to get a solid night's sleep. I had to lie flat on my back, slightly propped up, something I was not used to at all, being a side or stomach sleeper. This new position left my back feeling wicked tight, with layers of knots along it. I wanted to get a massage but couldn't figure out how to do that if I couldn't be on my stomach or lie against a massage chair, putting weight on my chest. Still, my pain was now tolerable enough for Tylenol to handle it, and no more pain medicine also meant no more migraines. I started stretching lightly and icing my back. Because my chest muscles were essentially shut down, my back had taken over, and it was on fire.

Kimberly arrived just after lunch, bearing all sorts of gluten-free and healthy foods. I didn't tolerate gluten well and limited the amount I ate. Kimberly was also very careful about her diet, so she had packed all sorts of goodies. Some delicious and others...

Chips, dips, gluten-free animal crackers—which were disgusting, by the way—yummy cookie dough dip she made from chickpeas, and my favorite...buffalo cheese curds! Cheese curds may not have made the healthy list, but this Syracuse girl loved anything buffalo-flavored!

Our first girls' night together we spent on the couch, watching movies, as I drifted in and out of sleep, granting her creepy wish of watching me do that.

Monday morning the kids had school. Kimberly and Brian helped get them up and ready for the day as I took my time getting out of bed. My pain was still the worst when getting up and down, and I certainly wasn't ready to hop out of bed just yet. My drains were really irritating me too, making me very grumpy, and I was pretty sure everyone noticed. Each time I sat up, I had to rely on my core and legs to avoid pushing off my arms. My chest was so tender and the drain sites, which were located on either side, allowing my arms to occasionally rub against them, were stinging and pulling. They were annoying, and I couldn't wait to get them out, hopefully the next day at my one-week follow-up.

Kimberly was so helpful during her visit, running the kids wherever they needed to go, making meals, and keeping me company. It was a huge load off, having her there with me, allowing me more time to stay focused on getting well again.

My one-week follow-up appointment fell on Kimberly's last day with me. Before she headed home, she would take me to the plastic surgeon's office. Knowing I'd had enough of my drains, she came up with a brilliant plan: "Why don't we fill the bulbs of your drains with glitter or something?" she said in a maniacal manner.

"Oh my God, that would be hilarious!"

I agreed to do it to prank the nurses and doctor, but we kept none of that devil dust in my house, so we decided to use food coloring instead.

"What color should we use?" I asked Collin, to let him share in our antics.

"Blue!" he quickly chose. "Then you can make them think you turned into Smurfette!"

"Okay, blue it is!" I agreed and began cleaning out the bulbs. Collin giggled with excitement and handed me the blue food coloring. A few drops of dye, a little bit of water, and the deed was done: I was Smurfette!

When we arrived at the doctor's office, I headed back to the examining room with Kimberly and one of the nurses. I had noticed my doctor at the desk, writing notes. With several staff and nurses surrounding us, I decided this was the best time for our little prank.

"Excuse me, Doctor, but could you please take a look at this? Is this normal?" I questioned as I stood, holding each bulb of my drains filled with blue water.

He paused for a moment, smiled, and laughed as he asked, "Valerie, what did you do?"

When we told him, the entire office started roaring. One of the nurses even took out a camera to take a picture.

The doctor followed me and my blue bulbs into the examining room, where he conducted a brief checkup. He was pleased to learn that I was off the pain medication and reassured me that I was healing just as I should be.

"Everything looks great, Valerie, but you're still dispensing too much fluid. We are going to have to keep the drains in for now."

Hearing that was disappointing, crushing the lightness of the mood we had created with our prank. I'd had my heart set on getting them out, and to learn that wouldn't be the case plain sucked, but I trusted him. I thanked the doctor for his time and went to the front desk with Kimberly to make my next appointment. Hopefully the drains would come out then.

Later, Kimberly started back home to her family in Syracuse. In her absence, Pat returned to help for a couple of days until my sister could come. At first I wasn't sure if I would need Monica to help, but by now I had surrendered to the fact that I needed all the help I could get. That became very apparent to me when, on the first day I was home from the hospital, I tried to open a bottle of water and couldn't. I literally had zero strength to unscrew the plastic cap. Every little movement seemed to radiate pain throughout my chest.

Monica hopped on a train to spend the next four days helping where she could. Pat drove out to the train station in Poughkeepsie, about forty-five minutes from our home, to pick up my sister. I couldn't wait for her to get here. She gave the *best* massages, and my back was still all knotted up.

On the way to pick up my sis, Pat dropped me off downtown. I'd decided to treat myself by indulging in a hot stone foot treatment at a local salon and spa. I'd never had one before but had heard they were incredibly relaxing.

As I was enjoying my treatment and the attention my feet were receiving, the owner of the spa walked over to say hello and offer encouragement to me. She was a member of the gym where I worked and was aware of why I had been out of work.

"Valerie, please, while you are here, let's shampoo and style your hair for you, my treat," she generously offered.

I hadn't been able to wash my own hair in over a week, let alone style it. Certainly, in all her years of experience, she had met women recovering from surgeries like mine. Offering some help in the area of grooming was very kind of her, so…I took her up on it.

I was continuing to soak my feet on the smooth stones that rested in a tub of warm water when I received a call from my father-in-law to inform me that my sister's train was eighty minutes late. Soon after his call, my sister texted me, "OMG, I feel so bad! We are running late, does Pat know? Is he mad?" I reassured her he was not.

Since retirement, Pat had a newfound outlook on life that didn't include rushing around. That was the beauty of retirement, he'd shared with us. His patience was not tested by Monica's train running late. Instead, he'd found a diner he'd frequented growing up and waited for her train, which arrived exactly eighty minutes late.

After my foot treatment was over, I walked over to the desk to pay. The spa manager had left a note saying it was her treat. "Better than flowers," she wrote. Blown away by the owner and the manager's continued generosity, I went downstairs to get my hair done.

There I was greeted by a pretty florid guy, and I mean that in the best way possible. He had no shortage of compliments for me. I was sure that was a part of his job, to make me feel relaxed and beautiful, but he appeared authentic about it anyway.

We started with a shampoo, and he massaged my scalp. I could've sat in his chair the entire day with his fingers massaging my head. Seriously, they should offer that as a spa treatment, having your hair shampooed and your scalp massaged.

Unfortunately, that only lasted a few minutes before we headed over to his station and he sat me down to ask me how I usually styled my hair. I answered, "With a baseball cap."

He laughed and began to perform his magic. When he was finished, he spun the chair around so I could take a look in the mirror. I absolutely loved it! Staring back at me was a reflection of myself I hadn't seen in a long while. I looked refreshed, I looked beautiful, and, most important, I *felt* beautiful—not like someone who'd just had a surgery that was making her feel less than her usual feminine self.

"Now, girl, this hair will get you three days, I promise! I have put in some product to hold the style and keep it from looking greasy. You're gonna get three days out of it, I swear!"

He went on to tell me that apparently I had the type of hair you can just talk to and it will listen. Well, I had never talked to my hair before. Hey, maybe it was like talking to a plant; maybe it needed the same positive affirmations to flourish.

I left the salon and spa feeling great, feeling more beautiful than ever, especially during such a vulnerable time in my life. What wonderful people they all were for giving me that.

A few minutes after I was finished with my appointment, Brian swung by to pick me up. He pulled up right in front of the salon in his plow truck.

"Well, this should be interesting," I remarked. "I have no idea how I am going to get up into this thing."

"Wait a second." He got out of the truck and headed over to my side to lift me up into it. "You look gorgeous, Valerie."

I needed to hear him say that.

By the time we arrived home, Pat and Monica were waiting in the kitchen.

"Hey, we were just talking about you. Did you have a nice outing? How are you feeling?" Monica asked as she came over to give me a very, very gentle hug.

"I'm good and glad you're here. Now you and Pat can commence the changing of the guard over me!" I told both of them.

Monica had already begun taking over my care by pouring me a fresh glass of water and instructing me to go sit on the couch.

"Go on, go rest and I'll be right in to relax with you."

I followed my sister's orders and headed into the living room.

Monica, my older sister by eleven whole months, was everyone's caretaker. Whether it was being in charge of her own family, being the team mom, or the manager at her workplace, she took tremendous care of all those around her. The way she always put others first, paying attention to the finer details of what would make another person happy, reminded me a lot of our mom.

Growing up, we were very close during our elementary school years. We even started out in kindergarten together—in separate classrooms, but in the same grade. When I cried, *daily*, to go see my sister in the room next door, my mother and the school administration thought it may be best to have me wait another year to start. That decision turned out to be the right one, because it gave us each our own identity and friendships.

Later, in our teen years, we grew apart, naturally, as most siblings do. Fights about clothes—mostly me stealing hers—about time spent getting ready for school, and all the typical hormonal, bitchy, and annoying matters you would expect to come out from two teenage girls who shared a bedroom. We were different from each other, but we shared one thing in common: a mother who suffered deeply from anxiety and depression. It was something we never talked about when we were kids, or hardly ever as adults.

Now, our relationship continued to strengthen. Especially since losing our mom. Although we may have dealt with it differently, our pain was the same in so many ways. We shared the burden of knowing how our mother died, and what it felt like to live with a heart that ached with constant wondering. Wondering if our mom was at peace now. Wondering if she was still angry with us. Wondering if she was with Uncle Bill and Grandpa, and if she could see what was going on in our lives now. Wondering...

Wondering if she *really meant to do it.*

Anguish was our unfortunate bond.

Relationships are not cast in stone, and ours certainly had evolved. We were raised without a father, and now our mother was gone. From our original family, Monica and I were all that was left and we were willing to do whatever it took to preserve that.

Having her there with me gave me the closest possible feeling to the comfort our mother would have given me if she were alive, and in the few short days I spent with my sister, I soaked it all in.

Phase 3

Two weeks out from surgery and it was catching up with me. My drains were still in, but it was time for me to get back to work, at least my desk job anyway. I really had thought my drains would be out by now, but my body apparently had other plans. At first the doctor had told me seven to ten days. Everything I had read said seven to ten days, and most friends who'd had procedures that required drains confirmed the same thing. Almost fourteen days with these awful things wrapped inside my chest and sticking out the sides of my body, my patience was wearing very thin. They hurt so freaking bad. They were all wrapped up inside me and looked like ribs popping out of my chest wall. The ones in the center, right in my chest cavity, were the very worst. At times they felt like claws pulling at my skin. The tubes inserted right under my armpits were incredibly irritating. As if the digging pain in my chest and ribs wasn't enough, why not add a constant poking and burning sensation to the mix? And let's not forget when I accidentally caught the tubing on something like a doorknob and it tugged the drain away from my body...That was enough to send even the strongest person right up a wall. Speaking of a wall, I guess I had officially hit my proverbial one.

Oh, and brilliantly, I had slept with a heating pad the night before. I had such terrible rib pain and was desperate for some relief, so, against my better judgment as well as going against doctor's orders, I'd used heat to try to alleviate the pain. I fell asleep with the pad resting under my right scar—can't even say "breast" because there was not one there anymore—and woke to a pretty good burn that was now blistering because I couldn't feel the fucking sensation of a burning heating pad! So, yes, after noticing my stupid, dumb, ridiculous burn that morning while dressing for work, I'd had enough.

As I cautiously fumbled my way through preparing for work, Brian shouted from the bathroom, "Are you sure you are okay to drive?"

"I think so. I will be super careful," I responded uncertainly. Truthfully, I wasn't supposed to be driving until after the drains were removed, but I had convinced myself it was okay because my drive to work was only about three miles, with Collin's school along the way.

"Brian, I can drop Collin off if you can take Bailey to the bus stop. I am only going in for a few hours; then I have an appointment with my breast surgeon at eleven. Do you think you can drive me to that?"

"Yes, I'll pick you up at work, okay? Anything else?"

"One more thing: Please help me finish getting ready."

My process for getting ready for the day turned into a laborious one postsurgery. Finding a button-down shirt to hide my drains and having Brian do my hair, or at least try his best. The good news was, we were getting better at it. The first week it took us nearly two hours to get me ready for the day, and now we'd gotten it down to under one. We were becoming regular pros, although there was much improvement to be made in the hairstyling department. Today, a ponytail sufficed.

Thankfully, my son was becoming pretty self-sufficient. When Brian and I finished getting ready, we found Collin in the kitchen, waiting for me to take him to school. Brian and Bailey headed out shortly behind us.

Key in the ignition, I cautiously attempted to turn around to take a look behind me before backing out of the driveway, only to discover I couldn't do it. I was unable to twist my torso at all—it hurt too much. I imagined this was one of the reasons why the doctors had told me not to drive while the drains were in. I was forced to rely on my mirrors to guide me out, which I was *not* used to doing; usually I relied on looking out the rear window, as my mother taught me how to drive. Slowly, ever so carefully, I backed out of the driveway.

It was always so nice to be able to drive Collin to school. Our morning conversations were something I always looked forward to, a scheduled time to slow down, radio off, ears open, just talking— albeit a short conversation, because his school was only five minutes from our home. But it was five minutes of uninterrupted time that was ours alone.

"Mommy, I have to return the two books I have, and then I have one that I want to take out and read with you," Collin explained.

"You do? What is it called?" I looked in the rearview mirror to ask him.

"It's about a boy who enters a free-throw contest to win a million dollars. It's called *The Million Dollar Throw*. It's a long chapter book!" he proudly boasted. "If I bring it home, may we read it together tonight?" he eagerly asked me.

Remembering the promise I had made to him about the things we could do together as I recovered, I said, "Of course, we can definitely do that."

I pulled up to his school and reminded him to take the bus to the gym, where Daddy would pick him up.

"Bye, Mommy, love you."

"Love you, Collin. See you later. Make sure you bring that book home," I said, then continued my drive to work.

When I arrived I moved to step out of the car and *bam*! My motherf'ing right drain caught on the shifter. "FUUUUUUUCK ME!" I groaned from inside the car so no one walking into the gym would look over to see stupid, pathetic me going back into work when clearly I should have stayed home.

My day continued on with business as usual, except for the lovely gift bag on my desk, which I hadn't noticed when I first walked into the office. It was from my boss and his family. The card was handmade by his twin boys, who were the same age as Collin. "Feel better!" it read, and they had both signed their names with love. It brought a smile to my face and helped to lift my dwindling spirits.

My office was empty. Everyone was out on the gym floor, working out, teaching class, or training. I sat at my desk, logged on to my computer and began working on the programming calendar for March. A few moments later the owner walked into my office. He was one of the investors in the gym. At eighty-five years old, he was an incredibly accomplished man with a wealth not only measured in money but also in life experience.

"Good morning Valerie! It is *so* nice to see you here, let me tell you!" he exclaimed as he walked over to give me a hug. Then he remembered. "I can't hug you yet, but I'll blow you a kiss," he said, which he did as he reached for my hand. He told me how sorry he was that I had to go through this and that he had been thinking about me.

His sincerity made me emotional. A lump formed in my throat and quickly swelled as I began to tear up. Just then, my boss walked into the office. Fortunately, he was a great friend who knew me well enough to see he needed to lighten the mood.

"What, did you tell her we already found her replacement while she was gone?" he teased. We all laughed at his wiseass remark and changed the subject to filling me in on what I'd missed in the past two weeks.

Our meeting was brief, and then my boss went out to check on the gym floor. As he exited, he looked back and said, "Good to have you back, kid."

Trying to sit without proper back support was killing me—still no relief from my back pain. Right below my right shoulder blade was a knot that felt about the size of a golf ball. The rest of my back was pretty tight and knotted up, but this one spot in particular was so painful that it distracted me from getting my work done. Nine thirty—one hour until Brian would be here to pick me up for my follow-up appointment with my breast surgeon. Maybe I could find one of those massage balls to place behind my shoulder to make sitting tolerable.

I decided to leave my desk and go out to the gym floor to locate a ball for my back. While walking the floor, I saw my team members, as well as members of the gym. By the way I was greeted, you would think some of them imagined I was away on a glorious vacation somewhere, although others knew the reason for my absence. Those who knew offered smiles, well wishes, and full support. Walking the floor and not hiding in my office was the relief I needed. Saying hello to everyone and absorbing their love gave me the boost I needed to go back into the office to finish the March calendar.

As promised, Brian arrived at ten thirty to pick me up for my appointment, which was the quickest one to date. No more than five minutes. The doctor looked at my chest briefly, then said she would see me in six months. That was it? Okay, it sounded like a legit plan to me. She explained that all my follow-up from that point on would be with the plastic surgeon. Hopefully at my next one with him, he would remove my drains, but I was not holding my breath.

Phase 4

I had those drains in for eighteen days. I prayed this follow-up would finally be the day the plastic surgeon would yank them out. I went to work earlier for a few hours and noticed even though I was pretty sedentary, just sitting at my desk, I was still draining a lot of fluid. So when I went home to get ready for my appointment with the doctor, I decided to call his office first before heading there. I didn't want to waste anyone's time by going in only for him to send me home without pulling out the drains, and I certainly wanted no part in any false hope for getting them out.

Over the phone I explained to the nurse how much fluid I was still losing, but she told me to come anyway. I anxiously waited for Trish to pick me up. She was my chauffeur for the day and still performed the very delicate task of documenting my progress.

As we drove to the appointment, Trish was very careful not to go too fast or hit any potholes along the way. I knew she was being extra cautious with me in the car, and I was appreciative. I still felt sore, but more than anything, I was nervous despite everyone—including the doctor, who I trusted—telling me that it didn't hurt to have the drains out. Well, seeing as anytime I asked anyone else how it was to have drains removed, they collectively chose the word "yank" to describe it, one could understand my hesitation.

We arrived on time for my three o'clock appointment, checked in, filled out more paperwork, and waited.

Trish and I began talking about our daughters, hers being the same age as Bailey. Both girls were very involved with performance arts, so we had a lot in common in that aspect. They also attended the same middle school.

Idly chatting away, I became aware we had been waiting for a while now, so I checked my phone. Three thirty—we had been waiting for thirty minutes already. I was aware of the time mostly because Trish was doing me a favor by being there and had a family to get home to. I walked up to the front desk and saw the receptionist was busy on the phone, but she waved me over anyway. "Half an hour behind," she wrote on a Post-it; obviously she knew what I was going to ask. I smiled and returned to my seat.

"Should only be a few more minutes; she said he is running a half hour late," I let Trish know.

"No prob. You doing okay?" she asked, sensing my nervousness.

"Yes. I just want to get this over with, and I really hope they pull the drains out today."

A few moments later my name was called, and Trish and I were led to the examining room.

"Oh, this is going to be a fun appointment, you brought a photographer with you and everything!" the nurse said with a smile. By now, Trish had been to the office with me a few times. The people there were used to seeing her with me and were very supportive of the reason behind it.

Trish began discreetly taking photos. "The doctor is going to remove the drains today," the nurse assured me as she began to set up the table, placing sterilized equipment on the metal table next to the examining chair I reclined on. While I was relieved when the nurse said that, my nerves started to set in again.

"Hey, Valerie, how are you feeling?" the doctor asked, a huge smile on his face as he entered the room.

"Good, anxious to get these out," I answered, pointing to my sides.

He examined all four of my surgical sites, the two long incisions across my chest and the two drain sites.

"You are really healing beautifully, Valerie. I am going to start with the right side and remove the stitches across your chest. It shouldn't hurt, but tell me if you feel anything. After that, I will remove the drain on that side."

After my stitches were taken out—painlessly—he instructed me, "Okay, take a deep breath in, now breathe out…"

Yank…the drain was out!

"That's it? That was it? You're done with that side?" I asked in amazement. It hadn't hurt at all. The left side went just as smoothly. As I looked over to the table where the doctor had placed both sets of drains, I was so surprised at the sheer length of them. I couldn't believe all of that had been wrapped up inside my chest. I was so relieved to have them the hell out of my body.

When he was finished, he placed Silvadene cream and gauze over all four surgical areas, then reviewed the directions on what to do at home so I would continue to heal properly. He also gave me the green light to start doing some nonimpact cardio such as the recumbent bike and walking, along with range-of-motion exercises to prevent my shoulders from becoming stiff. Lifting was still off-limits, as were pushing and pulling. The most exciting news I received during the visit was that my first boob fill would be on March 14. Fourteen, my family's lucky number—this must be a good sign! (Fourteen had been a lucky number for me ever since I could remember. It was the number I would choose for almost all my jerseys when I played soccer in high school, and I passed on the tradition to my son, who did the same when he first started playing baseball. And, of course, May 14 was my mother's birthday.)

I returned home to find a note for me on the kitchen counter: *Took the kids down to the lake to go ice fishing, be back soon. xo, Brian.*

I was feeling so good, I decided to do something I shouldn't have. There was a glass I wanted located way up on the third shelf in our display cabinet in the kitchen. I thought to myself, *I bet with the tubes out, I can reach for that.*

At five feet two inches, I needed a little assistance reaching up that high, so I placed my right hand down on the counter and pushed off from it to reach for the glass with my left hand. Instantly, I felt a pain shoot up the right side of my chest.

Crap! That was a very bad idea. I hope I haven't hurt anything in that area. Last thing I need are any setbacks, I said to myself and promptly headed into the bathroom to check my incisions. Everything seemed to be okay. Steady progress, I reminded myself, no pushing or pulling, doctor's orders, and for very good reasons.

By the time Brian and the kids returned home, it was dinnertime. They hardly got through the door before I burst out with my good news. "Guess what? I got my drains out today!"

Collin smiled, and without saying anything at all, he walked over to me and wrapped his arms around my sides to give me a loving but gentle hug, one that he'd waited eighteen days to give me. Bailey patiently waited her turn, then did the same.

I'd never realized until that moment what a barrier those drains were, not only for me, but for my family too. Now we could hug, albeit gently. Kids have a way of striking something wonderful deep inside you that no one else can. My children wrapping their arms around me did just that.

In the days after the drains were removed, I felt as if a little fluid was building up in my chest. Of course, I had already diagnosed myself with a seroma and could only think of Arnold Schwarzenegger in *Kindergarten Cop*: "It's not a tumor!" However, I really did think it was a seroma that had conveniently developed over the weekend when I was unable to call the doctor. Why does everything happen on a weekend? Seemed like any time my kids got sick, it was always on a Friday after five o'clock. My drains were in for eighteen days and truthfully probably could have been in longer. Not the fault of the doctor at all; most remove them in less time than that. My body was still just releasing a lot of fluid, and they anticipated this could happen. I called the office and the on-call doctor immediately got back to me telling me to set up an appointment for Monday morning so that my doctor could have a look at the swelling.

When Monday arrived, the doctor confirmed my suspicions, but assured me that it was only a small seroma. If my body didn't absorb the fluid on its own by the first boob fill, he would drain it.

Before leaving the examining room, he reminded me of the boob fill appointment, even though I didn't need reminding. I was *very* excited about it, hoping that the fill would leave me with two little bumps on my chest that would be another step forward in the restoration phase, allowing me to feel a little more like a woman again. Some women may feel flat and fabulous with nothing, but right now, physically, all I felt was scarred and disfigured.

With reassurances from the doctor that I was continuing to heal, I decided the next day would be the one when I would get back in the saddle and spin again. Rebuilding my endurance was very important to me, especially if I wanted to get back to teaching spinning class or any of the other ones I coached. One-month postop, I would have to start nice and easy.

The following day, I waited until the gym was quiet. I entered the spinning studio, put my phone in the docking station, adjusted the volume, and found the playlist I made for my first ride. It consisted of all songs that spoke to me. As an instructor, when making a playlist for a class, I tended to choose a variety of music so there was always a little something for everyone. This time, I was sure to select only songs that motivated me, because I would be the only student in the room.

I made all the usual adjustments on my bike, with the exception of the handlebars. They needed to be higher than I usually rode to avoid hunching over and placing any unnecessary stress on my chest and arms. Music on, lights low, I started to pedal, warming up to Coldplay's "Speed of Sound." Anyone who knows me knows Coldplay is my all-time favorite band. I even had songs from their album *X & Y* playing in the labor and delivery room when I had both my children.

With no real plan in mind other than to see how it felt to ride the spinning versus the recumbent bike, where you had back support, I began my ride. Would I be able to stand and support myself on the bike? I slowly lifted myself off the saddle and began my first standing hill climb.

I can do this, I am *doing this*, I thought to myself, and although my first attempt out of the saddle lasted only a minute, I did it! I proceeded to try three more little standing rollers, each one minute in length, each time building my confidence. It felt empowering. I was determined not to let it bother me that before all this, I'd had the stamina to ride both standing and seated hill climbs for much longer. Just because I couldn't do it now didn't mean I wouldn't be able to again. In time, I would, and maybe, in some ways, I would be even stronger than before.

For the next thirty minutes I continued to run myself through a series of different drills I used as a spinning coach. Spinning was the first class I became certified to instruct and I'd led classes for over fifteen years. It was my favorite class to teach. Anxious to get back to coaching, I began to slowly start putting in the work. I looked down and saw that I was just shy of fourteen miles. Fatigue was setting in, but fourteen is my magic number, so I had to grab it.

My first return to the bike and it felt incredible. It was the closest I had felt to being myself since before I had my mastectomy.

It wasn't coming easy, but nothing worthwhile usually ever does. I'd made a promise to myself as I started exercising: never push through pain. There is a distinct difference between discomfort and pain, and I knew my body well enough to feel the difference. But that day I took back my physical power; the rest...would have to wait.

ELEVEN

Human Love

"Your flaws are perfect for the heart that's meant to love you."

~TRENT SHELTON, FOUNDER AND PRESIDENT OF REHABTIME

FOUR IN THE MORNING AND ANOTHER COLD SWEAT wakes me from my sleep. I dreamed of my mother, only the second time since her suicide. I was visiting her in an apartment she had just moved into. Apparently I had been living somewhere else, not Connecticut. In the dream we were standing in her kitchen, doing dishes together, talking about me moving back to Connecticut. This wasn't a flashback to an event that ever happened. All I could remember from my dream was an overall feeling of how wonderful it was just to be in her company again. Just the two of us, in her new kitchen, which she seemed very proud of. Both of us so happy to be spending time together. There she stood, smiling as she washed the dishes, telling me all about the new valance she'd ordered to place over the kitchen window. "I have always wanted a window right above the sink," she said. "I ordered a beautiful valance with a butterfly print." Those were the only words I remembered my mom speaking in the dream, but I was left with a feeling of loneliness, a craving for her very essence.

The essence of my mother. A woman who embodied love but struggled so hard to love herself.

I thought maybe if I closed my eyes, I would fall back asleep and go right back to her kitchen, back to the feeling only a mother can give a child, one of comfort and unconditional love.

With my eyes closed, I began imagining all the things I would say to her given the chance.

"Mom, I love you. Would you please show me how to make your swordfish recipe?" A dish she so often enjoyed making for us whenever we visited. Whenever I visited…did I visit enough? Toward the end, probably not.

Was that why she succumbed to the final symptom of her depression, her suicide? Because she felt isolated, unworthy, lonely? Or was it because she couldn't feel, or what she did feel was too much for her tender heart to handle any longer? I'll never know, because she didn't leave a fucking note. She left too soon to pen a note. Would a note even matter, or would I still wake in the middle of the night haunted by so many unanswered questions?

There was no returning to sleep, to her. I lay wide awake with a familiar ache in my stomach that heightened each time I allowed myself to think of my mom. Although my dream prompted me to become upset, I still wanted to dream of her; it was the only way to see her now, in my dreams.

God, I *missed* her. I missed her voice. The same voice I was sick of hearing at times growing up was now the one I ached for so desperately. The voice that screamed at me when she lost her patience was the same voice that softened when she knew I needed her. I resented that I couldn't pick up the phone and tell her about the appointment I had that day, my first boob fill. We would joke about how weird this whole thing was. *A boob fill appointment, what the heck is that?* she would tease. And she would offer to come with me, to drop everything if I needed her to. Then, after, we would go to lunch and maybe do a little shopping. We would have made a girls' day out of each of my appointments so that instead of dreading them, I would look forward to fun times with her.

It hurt. The pain of remembering her. The unbearable pain of knowing why she was not here was so tremendous, it physically became hard to breath. At times it felt like my lungs were literally collapsing, narrowing to a point of irreparable damage. There were seconds that turned into minutes, into hours and then days, when I could not recollect if I had taken a deep breath that day. Grief was changing my breathing to a shallow pattern that I wasn't sure I could return from.

My mind raced in the stillness. *Breathe, Valerie*, I tried to remind myself. *Just breathe. She is not here and any amount of wishing and praying for her will not bring her back.* Sometimes it was easier to let my logical mind take over because my heart was still broken.

Instead I got on with my day, placing my guardian angel worry stone in my pocket to bring with me to the doctor's office.

Soon Bailey would be up bright and early to do her hair. Five thirty in the morning her alarm sounded, reminding her it was time to straighten her beautiful curly hair, which drove her father nuts! "We shouldn't even allow her to use the straightener—it's ridiculous!" It was an argument Brian tried to win at least once a week, without being equipped with the knowledge of what it was like to be a teenage girl.

Growing up in the eighties allowed me to understand the importance of setting an early alarm to get ready for school. When I was Bailey's age, I needed the time to pump up the volume of my hair and, of course, hold it in place with enough Aqua Net hairspray to last through a six-hour school day or through a wind tunnel! And let's not forget the frosted pink lipstick and jelly bracelets. Brian thought he had it bad with one teenage girl in the house getting ready in the morning; my mother weathered two.

When Monica and I were in our early teens we each had our own bedroom with an archway door that opened in the center, leaving just enough space to chuck a hairbrush or curling iron through. Many mornings objects came flying through that archway, not always because one of us needed to borrow something!

Sure enough, right on time, Bailey's alarm clock rang. Moments later, still half asleep, she made her way into my room and slid into a little space on my bed. We started talking about my appointment, and I teased her about how she may not recognize me when she got home from school with my brand-new boobs. Our family used our odd sense of humor as much as we could, figuring that laughing was better than crying. So far it had proved to be a very useful coping mechanism in this situation.

"Boob fill?" she wondered. "That's soooo weird. How big are they going to fill you?"

"You know what I always say, go big or go home!" I teased in return, and she laughed, hopped out of my bed, and headed to her room to get to work on her gorgeous hair.

Brian and I arrived to an empty waiting room at the plastic surgeon's office, allowing them to call me right in. I was their first appointment of the day.

"Good morning, Mrs. Walsh. Come on back," a familiar voice called out to me. Brian and I followed the nurse into the examining room to wait there.

"Holy shit!" My eyes widened.

"What?" he asked me.

"Look over there, on the tray table." I drew his attention to two large needles filled with a clear fluid. "*That's what's going in me! Both of those babies right there!*"

The actual procedure was a bit odd, but should be relatively painless, as it was explained to me, especially with my surgeon. My doctor was very conservative and would not expand me too fast, so as not to overstretch my skin. The expanders in my chest were equipped with a fill port built into the front of the device. He'd use a magnet to find the port and access it with a needle. He assured me that the entire process should only take a few minutes. Today he would be putting in approximately 40 ccs of saline on each side, or whatever my skin could handle.

"Hi, Mrs. Walsh. Are you ready?" the doctor checked in with me as he walked over to the tray table to inspect everything already laid out for him.

"So ready!" nervous with excitement, I responded.

He reclined my chair and instructed his nurse to begin my prep. He took out a magnet shaped like a pen, ran it over my right breast, and located the port.

"That's so cool!" Brian exclaimed, as he watched the entire process in amazement.

Next he inserted the needle of saline and completed my very first fill. Other than a bit of pressure and a sensation of cold fluid, the procedure went as promised: painless. After the few seconds it took to fill my right side, he moved on to my left and repeated the process.

"That's it. You're all set until the next fill in a few weeks. Stop by the front desk on your way out, please, to make the next appointment," he instructed before leaving the room.

This was another step forward in my recovery. If things stayed at this rate, I should be done with the entire reconstruction by summer. *Hey, maybe I will be able to run a few races this summer!* I thought to myself.

A few short days after my first fill a stomach bug paid me a visit at the very inconvenient time of one in the morning. This time I was woken by nausea, not a dream. It came on so quickly. I ran into the bathroom, where I proceeded to be violently ill for the rest of the night.

By daybreak I had nothing left in me to throw up, so that was when the dry heaves ensued. What a cruel joke on a woman with expanders in her chest to start retching the way I had been for hours now. I slithered back to bed, where I slept on and off for hours until my fever finally broke, leaving me in another cold sweat. There was no way I could even try to keep anything down, and my head was pounding almost as loud as the gurgling sounds coming from my stomach. It was as if some sort of alien had invaded my body while I was napping! Bloated, cramping, and achy, I stayed in bed for the remainder of the day.

Thankfully the worst of the bug lasted only a few days, with plenty of time for me to feel well enough for my next breast appointment, which I was anxious to get to because I believed I'd pulled a muscle from vomiting. It was so tender, right beneath my right breast, an area that had been a bit of a nuisance since my first surgery, with tenderness from day one. Now I thought I may have really tweaked something. It almost felt like a rib was out of place.

One more appointment before my exchange surgery was my next fill. After this boob fill I would have to wait a minimum of one month before they could do the exchange surgery, when the doctor would take out the expanders and put in my implants. My gummy bear silicone implants were still a bizarre concept for me. I would be lying if I said there hadn't been moments along the way when I hated the way I looked. Right after my first fill I felt pretty good. Immediately it gave my breasts more of a smooth, round appearance. But within days the saline settled into uneven pockets and my breasts began to appear lumpy, rippled, and uneven. There was no breast tissue left in my chest, which caused certain areas to appear concave. They also hurt all the time—chronic rib pain and muscle soreness. All of that sometimes caused me to wonder if I might have been happier stopping at the mastectomy, without going through with the reconstruction. Now I could understand why some women chose to remain flat and fabulous. The phases continued to challenge me both physically and emotionally.

Because my last appointment went so easily, I decided to take myself to this one. As I entered the waiting room, I recognized a woman who used to live in our town. I hadn't seen her in years. We were pregnant at the same time with our daughters and Brian used to work with her first husband. Back then, we spent a lot of time together: dinner parties, playdates, all the usual activities that bring young mothers together. But when she divorced her husband and moved to another town, we eventually lost touch.

She was there with her mother and her three beautiful daughters: her oldest, who was the same age as Bailey, and her twin girls from her second marriage, who I had never met before. This was *not* a place you wanted to run into anyone you knew, certainly not another mother. Nervously, I asked her why she was there, although I didn't want the answer to be what I knew it likely was.

"I have breast cancer, triple negative. I am almost done with chemo, with one more treatment to go. This is a wig. Sorry, I don't want to cry," she explained to me, all in one breath, fighting back the tears.

"If you can't cry here, where can you cry?" I tried to comfort her.

We continued to talk about her treatments in soft voices, trying our best to remain out of earshot of her children, who were over in the corner coloring together. We discussed how she was handling everything, where she was living now, and how life— *other than the whole cancer thing*—was going. While we were deep in conversation, one of her twins walked over and handed me a picture without saying anything.

"It's beautiful. I love all the pretty colors you chose. It reminds me of spring," I said to her, smiled, and handed it back.

"It's for you," she said shyly before going off to color some more with her sister.

"Hey, you're going to be just fine, okay?" I left my friend with a big hug and what little reassurance I could provide.

How the hell did I know that? Who was I to say such a thing? But I had to choose hope. Without it, we are left with the unthinkable. Later I Googled "Triple Negative Breast Cancer" while waiting for Collin at the bus stop, which made me lose it entirely in the car, asking myself why a beautiful young mother had to face the unknown, whether or not she would be there to raise her girls. It brought me right back to the feelings I'd had after being diagnosed with thyroid cancer, when Bailey was a baby, questioning whether I would be alive to see her grow up.

Truthfully, when the woman revealed her diagnosis, I couldn't help but feel somewhat guilty admitting to her that I was there for preventive measures. Feelings of not having the "right" to complain or that I may have had it "easier" weighed heavily on my heart.

Why me? Why her? How dare I feel frustrated or sorry for myself that my boobs no longer looked normal to me? Who the hell was I to complain about a little rib pain, or that I couldn't exercise just then the way I was accustomed to? My feelings seemed so *less than.*

I began to compare, a dangerous and toxic thing to do to myself. While my brain logically knew that just because someone was going through something different or even more difficult, it didn't mean my situation was any less than, my heart felt differently. Since the beginning of my diagnosis, I had struggled with feelings of guilt and shame.

Now there I was, asking what seemed to be a very frivolous question of myself: How much should I allow the doctor to fill at this appointment? The doctor added a small amount at first, reminding me what we'd discussed at the very beginning: that it may take somewhere around three fills to get my boobs to the size I was comfortable with. They do say the third time's the charm, and that just may be the case now, when I was not pleased with the way they looked. To me, they appeared wide, not full. So, I shared my concerns with my doctor.

He listened to my thoughts, then asked me to stand in front of the mirror after he had added the first small amount. With both of our eyes now intent on my body, he said, "I see what you mean. I promise I will be selecting a smaller implant and your breasts will not look like they do now, not as wide. If we go with another fill today, you will be a full B, just as you wanted."

Pleased with that information, I agreed to continue. The nurse began to prepare the syringes for another fill. When that was done, he said his surgical coordinator would call me in a few days to set up my appointments, preparing me for my final surgery, the exchange surgery.

As promised, a few days later I received the much-anticipated phone call, and the exchange surgery was set for Tuesday, June 10, 2014. It was finally coming, the last phase of the long reconstructive process. I was nearing the end of my path to physical healing.

I spent most of the time leading up to this surgery doing all the things I was used to. Keeping busy with work and the kids' schedules and getting in a few easy workouts. The family filled our weekends with fun things to look forward to, like the flea market.

On a beautiful Sunday morning in May, Brian and I and the kids woke up at the crack of dawn to get to the flea market early, anticipating it would be very busy. When we parked the car and started walking toward the entry, Collin complained he was cold. "Mom, I think I left my sweatshirt in the car," he said.

"Okay, you guys head inside. I'll go back and get it," I offered.

There *was* a chill in the air, so I jogged back to the car to warm up a bit, which proved to be a stupid move. Suddenly a sharp, shooting pain under my right rib stopped me in my tracks. This was the same area where I had been having pain on and off since my mastectomy. The same area, but this time the pain seemed to be much worse. The pain was so intense, it hurt even to walk.

I slowly made my way to the car for the sweatshirt, then back toward Brian. Before I could make it to him, he came running over.

He noticed right away that something was wrong. "What is it?" he asked, concern in his voice.

I whispered so Collin couldn't hear me, "Same side. It hurts *so* bad. I really don't think I can walk around."

Now even more worried, he asked me if I wanted to go home. "No, we'll just walk slowly and look around." But about two aisles in, I found a picnic table where I planted myself for the next hour, while Brian and the kids lingered about, hunting for treasures. They returned with two baseball cards for Collin—the great Randy Johnson and Barry Bonds—and Bailey had found some antique jewelry. With those excellent finds, we decided to call it quits. By that time we needed to get ready to head to my grandmother's apartment anyway, where we were celebrating her eighty-seventh birthday.

We'd planned to take my grandmother out for brunch per her request. I loved going to visit her. The town where she lived now, Kent, Connecticut, was absolutely adorable. The quaint little town held many shops and restaurants. It was a well-known tourist area, especially for motorcycle riders and outdoor enthusiasts. Bikers and hikers alike stopped in Kent to get a bite to eat or a cup of coffee.

My gram had chosen a local diner for her birthday brunch.

"Valerie, call me when you're about five minutes away so I can wait for you out front," she had instructed me. Her legs were giving her a bit of trouble—neuropathy. She never liked asking for help—well, not from me anyway. A very proud and independent woman, she always insisted on making her own way out to the front of her building so as not to put us out. That was the way she felt, but I never minded. I especially enjoyed having her company in the absence of my mother.

At brunch the kids were very excited to have their great-grandmother open the gift we'd picked out together, a garden stone with a beautiful cardinal on it. Cardinals reminded my grandmother of my grandpa. It was one of his favorite birds. Whenever one flew near, she was certain it was a sign that he was paying her a visit. It was a nice symbol. I understood her looking for those signs of him, as I had come to have my own for my mother. She had her cardinals; I had my angel stone and feathers.

"You forgot to open the card," Collin reminded her. Bailey handed their great-grandmother the card.

Shoebox messages never disappoint, and this one didn't either. The sassy old lady on the front of the card reminded me of my grandmother, as did her wise-ass remarks written inside. My gram loved it almost as much as I enjoyed finding the perfect one to make her laugh, which she did, and then she moved on to decide what to order for her birthday meal.

After we ate, we headed over to her apartment to visit some more. By this point I could no longer hide the fact that I was in pain from my stupid move jogging back to the car. As a former nurse, it was not long before my grandmother became aware that I was not comfortable.

"What is it, Valerie? Do you not feel good?" She lovingly checked in with me. Then, when I explained what had happened, her voice became firmer, "Oh, you never sit still. Go home and stay put, would ya?" she scolded me, and I agreed. It was time for me to get some rest.

"Bye, Gram. I you, me too. I'll call you tomorrow to let you know what the doctor says. I am sure everything is fine—I probably just overdid it a bit."

"Slow down and you'll get done a lot quicker, kid." This was something my grandmother advised me of often, and she was usually right.

Upon arriving at home, I did just as my grandmother instructed, went to bed and stayed put.

The next morning I called the doctor first thing and he got me right in. He checked out the area and assured me it was nothing more than a bone bruise, along with some muscle spasms between my ribs. He showed me how to massage out the trigger points and promised me that although it was painful, nothing was seriously wrong. This type of pain, unfortunately, was pretty common. One month more with these wretched expanders. I felt just the way teenagers feel about getting their braces off their teeth!

Before leaving the doctor's office, I saw I had a text from Trish, who told me to check my email ASAP. She was going to send me a sensitive photo and wanted to "warn" me about it. I rushed to the car to open the email. I was so curious, I could not wait the twenty-minute drive home to see it.

The picture started to slowly download and then, there it was…A black-and-white photo of my husband and me. Brian was standing behind me with his arms wrapped around my body with such strength. His embrace framed my chest. My naked, scarred chest, postmastectomy and prefill. The image did not show our faces, just my battered, broken body, held by our unbroken bond.

In this image I saw love and hardship. Love that was human, messy, unperfect, and authentic. Fucked-up, real-life problems and how we were learning to navigate through them, by holding on.

I just had to hold on a little longer. *Hold on, darling, someday you will float as light as a feather through life again.*

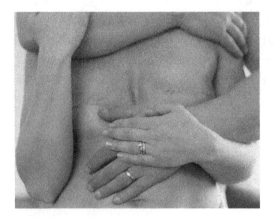

TWELVE

Physical Healing, Final Phase

"Feathers appear when angels are near."

~NATIVE AMERICAN SYMBOLISM

May 11, 2014—Mother's Day

As I pulled into the cemetery, I felt my stomach begin to flutter. A feeling of unsettlement was gradually taking me over, right down to my core. All day I had avoided coming to the cemetery, where my mother's body was laid to rest. Now, it was just me and her— well, her headstone anyway. My first Mother's Day without my mom and I couldn't feel her anywhere, certainly not there.

I looked down vacantly at the two graves, one for my mom, the other for my uncle Bill, her brother. Before I took my spot on the damp grass, I scoped the scene, hoping there were no other visitors. I wanted privacy. Some time to speak out loud to my mom in good faith, in case she actually heard me this time. And, of course, I didn't want anyone to witness me talking to myself, although I was sure the only people who would be here on Mother's Day were possibly doing the same.

Relieved to find no one else in sight, I mindlessly started pulling up the pieces of grass that crept through the white stones covering the graves until I realized that was yet another distraction. Every day I tried to avoid what was too painful for me to face. My mother died by suicide, and I was saying "Happy Mother's Day" to a woman who had been anything but happy. She was sick and felt isolated; suicide was just the final symptom of her massive depression. Now it was me and her headstone and, just beneath me, her body. But where was her spirit? Was she at peace?

So many times I had prayed that if she *was* now at peace and free from her pain, I could bear all the pain left for us now. I placed the single hydrangea I'd brought as a gift on her grave, kissed her headstone, and whispered to her softly, "Happy Mother's Day, Mom. I wish you were here; I miss you so much," and then…

I waited.

Although I still felt it was useless, I waited for anything that might prove to me that somehow spiritually she was whole again. Maybe the wind, a bird, the smell of lavender, or maybe…a feather.

"Please, Mom, please, show me something."

When nothing came, I continued my pleading: "Why can't you show me something solid? Something I would without a doubt, no question, know is from you! When I get back into the car, if I turn on the radio and hear Fleetwood Mac, or Journey, or even that song, 'Lido,' then I'll know you were listening. I promise, I'll be okay with the fact that you are gone as long as I know you are okay, that you are having a nice day today. I want to know that when Collin gets nervous up at bat, you are the one who is helping to calm his fears. I need to know that you saw how beautifully Bailey danced in the spring recital last night. Did you see her? She was amazing! Why can't you come to me? I ask every day…where are you? God damn it, where the fuck are you? Please. Please show me something…please."

Nothing.

Maybe if I stayed a little longer, I would see something, or *feel* her. Instead, a sickening anxiety found its way into my heart and stomach. The peace that surpassed all understanding that we as Christians prayed for—that was the peace I so desperately needed to feel. My mind knew it wasn't my mother's responsibility to give it to me, but my heart didn't. Truthfully, my heart hadn't felt any calm since the moments before I was floating in Candlewood Lake, the moments before she drew her last breath.

The pain of losing my mother for all the reasons and answers I was so desperately searching for overshadowed any amount of pain I felt from losing my breasts. She didn't die naturally, painlessly, or surrounded by family, although I prayed she went as "gently into the night" as possible. It was all fucked up, and I was having a very hard time making any sense out of it.

Bailey and Collin made sure I had a nice Mother's Day, despite my efforts to sabotage it myself with that shitty visit to the cemetery. Sure, I could have continued to dwell on the agony I'd felt at her graveside, but my kids didn't deserve that, nor did I. Being the mother of two amazing kids was reason enough to be happy. We went to see Bailey dance in her second performance and continued to celebrate at brunch with my mother-in-law.

Until I lost my mother, I never knew it was possible to hate an entire month, but now…I hated May. It held a painful reminder of her on Mother's Day, followed by her birthday, and finished off with the date of her suicide. This May she would have been sixty years old.

My sister and I had planned to do a girls' weekend for our mother's sixtieth. We would go to the spa, pamper ourselves, then head back to her house for movies, good food, and more relaxation. Why had we waited? We shouldn't have waited, but that's what we all do, right? We wait. We wait for the perfect time, for enough money, for signs…we wait. Until one day life smacks you right in the face with a what-the-fuck-were-you-waiting-for? reminder. That was what my mother's sixtieth birthday was to me—a huge reminder that I shouldn't have waited.

We should have been on our spa weekend—my mother, my sister, and me, pampering ourselves, spending some much-needed girl time together. Why had we waited for her to turn sixty? Why had I waited to visit her? I should have packed a bag and headed straight to see her after our last phone call. I knew she wasn't doing well. But I was too busy with my own stuff, right? How could I have cast my own mother aside?

On the day of my mother's birthday, I decided not to go to the cemetery and set myself up for yet another disappointing visit. We are designed to move away from things that are unpleasant and toward enjoyment, and I had become the master of staying busy enough to avoid any feelings that I wasn't willing to face. So, I headed to the park for an easy jog.

Harrybrooke Park was a place I often went to jog or walk. It was not far from the gym, making it a very convenient place to duck out to during a break between classes and clients.

This time I changed my route, venturing up a different path along the water. On the path, scattered all the way at the top of the hill, I began to find feathers. At first I thought nothing of it; then I remembered a story my good friend Gail had shared with me about finding feathers after her mother died.

Gail was one of the first people I called when I learned my mother had died. I can't explain why. Something just told me to call her. Gail was my daughter's physical therapist in 2011, after her foot surgery. During that time our family became very close. She was "Aunt Gail" to my kids. To me, she was a friend and someone I considered a spiritual guide.

One night, after a dinner out, we went back to her home to continue our visit. There, I noticed she had a collection of beautiful feathers. She explained how she found them in the strangest places and began collecting them. Gail told me that Native Americans believe that "feathers appear when angels are near."

As I continued up the path and started seeing more and more feathers, I stopped running and began picking up every one I found along the way, on my mother's birthday. From that day on I began my own collection of feathers in hopes of finding peace.

June 10, 2014—Exchange Surgery Day

Both Brian and Trish came with me for my exchange surgery. Trish wanted to continue to document this final phase, and Brian was there to calm my nerves.

We arrived nice and early, as instructed, allowing enough time to fill out the standard paperwork I could now complete with my eyes closed. Soon after, I was called in to the preop room.

The doctor was already there and began reassuring us all that this procedure would be nothing like the eight-hour mastectomy. He anticipated this would take about three hours and I would not have to stay the night. The nurse informed Brian and Trish that they would be allowed to stay with me until it was time for me to move into the operating room.

From there, things began to move pretty quickly. It looked like my surgery would start right on time, at nine in the morning.

Next, the anesthesiologist entered to start my IV. He placed it into my right forearm. I had never had one there before but didn't question it. He told me I was all set and the nurse would be in soon to get me for surgery.

As I was waiting, I began to feel my right forearm balloon up with pressure; it felt like the fluid was going directly into my arm, not my vein. When the nurse arrived for me, I showed her my arm. I could see by the look on her face she didn't like what she saw. She asked me if I was okay to stand and walk to the operating room so they could fix the IV right away. I stood up feeling a little shaky but was able to steady myself.

I gave a quick hug and kiss to Brian and Trish and headed down the hall to the operating room, where the anesthesiologist attempted to fix the IV.

"What do you do for work, Valerie?" he asked, obviously trying to distract me from the pain of his several attempts to restart the IV.

"I work at a gym, teach classes, and train people for a living," I replied.

"Oh yeah? That's cool. I am a road biker myself," he shared with me, continuing to get the IV in.

By the fourth stab and failed attempt, I reminded him of what I did for a living and told him I was going to invite him on a ride, the hilliest route I could find, and kick his ass! I was done. Thankfully, so was he; on the fifth attempt he was successful.

When I awoke from surgery, the first things I noticed were the four veins that were blown out from the failed IV attempts on both my right and left arms. I also saw it was after three o'clock. I asked the nurse in the recovery room how long the operation had taken.

"Everything went great, Valerie. It took a little bit longer because your plastic surgeon is a perfectionist."

I certainly couldn't argue with that, but I wanted to know where Brian was. He had expected me to be out of the operating room by noon. Moments later he came into the recovery room to join me.

"I was starting to get really worried until your surgeon finally came out to tell me everything went fine. I guess it took longer for whatever reason. You okay?" he asked, concerned.

"I am. My arms are sore," I said, raising my arms to show him the blown-out veins. Other than that, I also noticed my neck and shoulders were tight from the way I assumed they'd needed to position me on the operating table, again laid out like the letter t.

Soon after coming to, I remembered what was happening today too. Collin's in-house championship baseball game! "We have to get home so at least you can go, Brian!" There was no way I could possibly make the game, but if they released me by five o'clock, Brian could get there on time.

A short time later a nurse popped in to check on me, and I did my best to try to convince her we needed to get out of there. When I told her why, she was very understanding. "Well, then, let's get things moving along so we can get you home. I know how important this stuff is; I have three children, although they are all grown now." She sped up the discharge process for us to get out of there as quickly as possible.

Brian was able to get to Collin's game on time, where his team took second place in the championship game. When they returned home, Collin rushed into my bedroom to show me the trophy he received. Proudly, he explained, "Look, Mom, it's a baseball glove, and you know what's really cool about it? It can hold my first homerun ball when I catch it!"

"That *is* really cool, Collin," I answered, and then said good night to both kids so I could rest.

In the weeks following my surgery, my recovery continued very smoothly, much more easily than the initial surgery. By the end of August 2014, the doctor gave me full clearance to go back to my normal activities, but to continue to be cautious when it came to pushing and pulling for a little while longer. Slowly, I began to regain the physical strength I lost during the past year. However, emotionally…I was still drowning.

THIRTEEN

History Repeats Itself

"Sometimes shattered pieces never go back together the same way they did before, no matter how hard you try"

~VALERIE WALSH

Summer 2015

It had been years since I had my last drink and only one year since my breast surgery. I felt like I had paid my dues, so to speak, but where was it getting me? Nowhere. Lost, I felt myself returning to my old familiar friend, grief. That summer I would become reacquainted with another customary mode of coping—alcohol.

"Mom, may I go over to my friend's house instead of the beach party?" Collin asked. He was now ten years old and full of energy that required hours of playing outside, which I happily supported.

"Sure. I'll drop you off before I head down to the picnic. Start getting ready and remember to put on sunscreen!" I was the queen of sunscreen, going through gallons of it, aiming to protect my fair children's gorgeous porcelain skin.

Each year our lake community held an annual picnic. It was an event everyone looked forward to, a chance for our neighbors to get together with family and friends to kick off the summer. Collin usually joined us, but this year, apparently, he'd made plans with buddies of his. Bailey and Brian were already down at the beach, waiting for me to join them as soon as I dropped Collin off.

We lived on top of a mountain—literally, the last house at the very top. On our way down the hill to the main road, we passed one of our neighbors walking down to the beach.

"Hey, Mike, you need a ride?" I asked him. It was a sweltering day, and I could see he was soaked with sweat and breathing heavily.

"No, all good!" Mike replied with his signature smile across his face. "It's gorgeous out, so I decided to walk down. See you soon!"

Collin and I drove on to his friend's house. Moments after I dropped him off, my cell phone rang.

"Valerie, oh my God. Are you driving still?" It was Brian on the other end of the line.

"Yeah, why? What's up?" I answered. "I can talk."

"It's Mike. They're working on him now. It's not good. I think he's having a heart attack. They have the defibrillator on him, but they've already tried three times. He walked down here and then literally, like a few minutes later, collapsed. Right in front of everyone."

I pulled the car over and sat in disbelief. I had just talked to Mike and offered him a ride. He was smiling, happy, ready to party. He was only forty-eight. There was no way things could be that serious, could it?

"Valerie, it's bad. Really bad. They're taking him to the hospital now."

I decided not to go to the beach, but to the hospital instead. There, I saw Mike's wife, son, and a few close friends, all in shock and sobbing. I didn't know how I could help or what I could say. In truth, there was nothing I *could* do. Mike's wife had enough people surrounding her, holding her up in anticipation of the possibility that the most horrific news was about to be delivered.

Ultimately, they were unable to revive him. Mike passed from a massive heart attack.

A few short days later, as a community, we laid Mike to rest. His wife felt it was appropriate to have a celebration of his life with a beach party following the church ceremony and burial. Mike would have wanted it that way. He was well-loved in our community and always enjoyed his time with friends and family at our beach.

I remember that afternoon, the day of his celebration, and the decision I made to start drinking again.

"Bri, I think I may have a few beers at the beach today."

"Are you sure? You've gone this long. I mean, I don't care, it's up to you."

Brian never questioned my reasons for drinking or stopping drinking. I had abstained from alcohol throughout our years together for a number of reasons, when we had our children, during their younger years, and, most recently, during my health scare.

"Yeah. I mean, if today has taught us anything, it's that life is short. Why am I putting all this pressure on myself not to drink? We aren't promised tomorrow. I just want to relax and enjoy myself with all of you." Even as I heard myself say those words out loud, I knew it was all a bunch of bullshit excuses to make myself feel better about the decision I was about to make.

There is a saying in my recovery program, a program I wouldn't find until September 17, 2017: "It's the first drink that gets me drunk." That was always the case for this alcoholic.

I cannot remember how many drinks I had that day, but I do remember that summer afternoon leading to a two-year battle down an old familiar road, only this time, it wasn't *fun* anymore.

In the years after I lost my mother, I developed unhealthy coping mechanisms, one of them being hanging on to my grief. That grief became the armor I wore for protection from getting hurt any further. I was afraid of letting love in. I felt unworthy of love, of peace. I had failed as a daughter, and I deserved to sit in my misery, and so…I did.

Outwardly, I appeared positive, strong, and present. All while, inwardly, I was anything but. What I showed on the outside was far from what I was battling on the inside.

I was available for everyone in my life: coaching the CORE Fitness Method, helping others through their tough times. I continued on as a personal trainer and fitness instructor, and professionally things were booming. Most people in any service-based industry will admit there are times when they feel as though they are a therapist. This was also true in my profession. For me, it was a tremendous honor to be able to help someone overcome a physical hurdle that almost always tied back to some sort of emotional burden he or she had been carrying around. Overcompensating, just as my own mother had, became my way too. If you asked me how I was, I would likely give the same answer every time: *Everything is fine*.

History was starting to repeat itself, and slowly I began to become more aware of what I was allowing into my life and what I was pushing away. However, I couldn't seem to help myself. There were many mornings I would literally stare in the mirror and wonder if I would ever be truly happy again. Times when I reminisced over pictures of me smiling and laughing with friends, questioning whether that girl would ever return.

When I took that first sip of beer in the summer of 2015, it gave me everything I remembered drinking could give me. That first sense of calm, the one I would feel before the storm it always eventually led to. It was a language I had come to understand, one that lured me in with everything I wanted to hear: I was pretty, charming, intelligent, and confident enough, *that* I *was enough*. Alcohol humored me like the fake friend you allow in your life for far too long.

I was a binge drinker. While I didn't drink often, when I did it was a lot. I never stopped at just one or two...I drank to get drunk, to fit into the "normal" atmosphere of whatever crowd I was trying to weave myself into.

From 2015 to 2017, my social anxiety seemed to heighten as a result of my unaddressed trauma. Alcohol, my usual crutch, which held me up in years past, was starting to affect me differently. During the first few drinks, I was able to lose myself and enjoy moments of joy only briefly. Most nights of heavy drinking with friends ended with me blacking out and waking the next morning filled with crippling anxiety. I didn't talk about this with anyone at the time. Alcohol was no longer lifting my spirits; it was literally *killing* them. Even though my body was showing me all the signs that I could no longer drink safely, I couldn't seem to stop on my own. I would work hard all week long—professionally, physically—be present as a mother, as a wife, as a coach so that when the weekend came, I felt as though I "deserved" to unwind. Like it was some kind of reward for just showing up. But it was far from a reward. It was a curse.

I used alcohol to help take the edge off areas in my life that I felt the most uncomfortable with, especially when it came to intimacy. Growing up with the worst of examples of men my mother chose to "love her" made it very difficult for me to trust as I began forming my own relationships. Allowing a man to get close to me physically was absolutely nerve-racking unless I had a buzz on. Looking back, I realized most of my physical relationships with boyfriends usually included a night of heavy drinking. That was also how I lost my virginity. At the age of eighteen I was raped during a night of heavy drinking, a horrific night I blocked out of my memory for many years, remembering only faint moments of asking the boy to "please stop." He was a boy I knew from high school, who had a reputation of taking advantage of girls. What remained imprinted in my brain was waking up the next morning, hungover, lying in my own blood, and him gone, along with my innocence and any concept of what consensual and loving sex should be like.

I was able to get away with drinking too much for so long because I was young and usually the person I was dating at the time drank just as much, if not more, than I did. Alcohol helped me to lose my inhibitions, to relax just enough to feel comfortable in my own skin.

By the time I met Brian, I had a pretty sturdy wall around me. My wall was built of bricks and mortar through years of witnessing my mother being mistreated by selfish, abusive men. Brian was the only man who broke through that wall and steadied my cautious nature when it came to believing that a man could truly love me—all of me.

When I turned back to alcohol in 2015, instead of drinking taking the edge off, it began to build my edges higher. Those edges I built as an adult eventually formed a barrier reminiscent of the one I put up as a young girl, a barrier to protect myself from further pain and disappointment.

For a while my surgery and the unaddressed grief of my mother's death started shaping me into a different person. When Brian tried to get physically close to me, I felt uneasy. Those same strong arms that once framed my brutally torn-up chest became the ones I was pushing away.

My mother's suicide changed me. It shattered any trust I had in other people, in relationships. All the work I'd put into allowing myself to finally trust again was gone. My pain was stuck deep down inside me, at a level too far to recognize at the time I was living with it.

So I was no longer the life of the party. Now drinking heightened whatever feelings I was working so hard to bury deep inside my tortured soul. Mostly…fear.

In August 2017 I traveled back home to Syracuse to celebrate with Kimberly. Her husband Eric was turning forty, and she was having a party for him at his favorite restaurant. It would be the first time I met a group of the close friends she had made over the years. Friends she had bragged to about me. Kimberly had painted a gracious picture of her best friend, Valerie, from Connecticut. She had talked about how positive and fun I was and was really looking forward to introducing her lifelong friend to her inner circle.

However, the woman who showed up that night was a shell of the one Kimberly remembered.

The night started out fun, beginning with introductions and a few sips of wine to try to take the edge off. As the evening—and the drinking—continued, the lighthearted conversations started to turn very dark. Somehow the topic of raising a teenage girl and mental illness arose, triggering a very defensive and dismal reaction in me. Instantly, Kimberly could see that my mood had changed. She tried her best to steer the awkward discussion to something more harmless, more appropriate for a birthday party, but I wouldn't let up. I moved on from the conversation eventually, but the damage was done. Needless to say, I left the party and, the next morning, woke to feelings of regret and shame over the way I had carried myself.

My visit left Kimberly very worried about my emotional well-being, and she wasn't alone...I was worried too. I started to realize I needed help.

I took my last drink on September 16, 2017. On September 17, 2017, I became sober by following a program that provided me with some of the tools I needed to help heal my wounded soul. The rest I found through returning to my roots.

FOURTEEN

Epic Simplicity

"From Mother Nature's roots, I will grow."

~VALERIE WALSH

MY PROBLEMS WERE NOT UNIQUE, BUT THEY WERE MINE. Whether I created them or they were brought on by unfair circumstances, they needed to be dealt with by understanding *why* I became the alcoholic I tried so desperately to avoid being.

Reconnecting to my spirit so my soul could heal came, for me, in the most available of all places, my own backyard.

I have always been an avid hiker and trail runner, but in sobriety my time spent in nature became different. The woods that were once only my playground for fitness became the place I would return to over and over to not only become physically stronger, but to restore my spiritual connection as well. This sacred time spent with Mother Nature allowed me to return my soul to a peaceful existence. Mother Nature granted me comfort in a way that my own mother once did, offering me grace, acceptance, and confidentiality. She was dependable, providing unwavering support whenever I needed to whisper—or scream—into the wind.

It was five o'clock on a warm summer morning in 2019, and my alarm rang relentlessly; it was time to get up and do the things that I knew I needed to do on a daily practice, to stay CORE strong.

"Turn that thing off! Why do you have it set so early and then press Snooze so many times?" Brian asked me this question every morning I set the alarm for the crack of dawn, and I answered him the same way I had for most of our years together: "I don't know. I thought I would get up right away."

Instead, I rolled out of bed with reluctance, but without the unwelcome guest that used to visit me most mornings.

My misery was gone, and dread was also no longer welcome in my home. I simply started paying attention to the work I needed to do to become spiritually fit. Whenever I trained for a physical challenge, I found a training guide and surrounded myself with like-minded people to help me stay accountable. The same thing needed to be done if I wanted to become spiritually fit as well.

It is often said that successful people simply have really good habits. The habits I incorporated into my daily routine included morning meditation—yes…sometimes at five in the morning, after hitting the Snooze button a few times—connecting with other alcoholics in recovery, who in many ways have become another group of CORE peeps for me to stay accountable to.

I also retreated into the woods almost daily. Nature became my church. Sometimes shared with others, while other times alone, but never lonely. That was different now too. My time alone was not a means to isolate and avoid social situations. It was rather a time for myself, to become grounded and connected to my roots, of who I am as a child of God. Each day during my morning meditation I would ask God to show me how to live my life with simplicity and calm, and to be of service.

Epic simplicity to do the next right thing. That was it. I did not have to solve the world's problems, nor try to figure out why my mom died by suicide. These were not my issues to solve. There were never any signs to show me any of this either, no matter how hard I begged. My answers all came in the moments I decided to surrender over all my fears, all my questions and doubts, to a power greater than myself, and in nature I could literally feel that power. The earth never laughed beneath my feet. Instead, it supported me so I could continue to grow.

My mother raised me to be a fighter, constantly picking up the pieces whenever life, or a man, knocked us down. So, for a long time the word "surrender," for me, meant "to quit." To give up, release control over a situation. Release control? For this type A gal, that was frankly the hardest fucking thing I have ever had to learn to do—abandon control.

I controlled everything from the time I woke up to the time my head hit the pillow, and then I even tried to control my thoughts, with little success. Schedules, menus, how our home was run, navigating teenage and adult drama, the list went on. For so many years I was the chess master of not only my life, but also the lives of my children, who were now nineteen and fourteen. For a very long time I remained a skilled player, moving around the individual pieces to ensure everyone was where he or she needed to be in life so he or she would not fall off the board. Until I finally realized the power of surrender.

It took me forty-four years to discover how to do that, and I am still learning more each day.

Everything that desecrated my soul—the alcohol, the fear, the dread, and every single thing that tried to shatter my core—it all had to be surrendered, and that took discipline. Just as my physical training did, my spiritual routines were a practiced discipline until one day they became a part of me.

Before sobriety, I was unable to break through to the surface and float gracefully through life, just as a feather does. My own self-will had stunted my spiritual growth until I was sick of spending my days grieving over things I could never change or find the answers to. Those questions about my mother's suicide are no longer piled up at my door. It is said that if you know love, you know pain. My mother loved me ferociously; therefore the pain left behind from her suicide was enormous. It took the time it took for me to learn how to face my pain, and to evolve from it and now use it to help others who are sick and suffering.

Time also allowed me to remember the many reasons I loved my mother. Eventually I was able to talk more about the way she cared for me. No, my childhood wasn't one that I would wish for my own children, but there certainly were periods-I could choose to remember, along with times I could choose to grow from: Remembering how my mother loved being my Girl Scout leader. The joy she took in planning any event involving her girls; from our birthday parties to school picnics, she was always there. The way she made butterscotch pudding, allowing it to cool on the counter for the perfect amount of time to form the skin on top, just moments before we would find our places in the living room to watch *Solid Gold*.

It was in the little things. The moments she likely thought of as just a mother's job, but that made me feel special, feel loved. It made me wonder if anyone ever told her just how special and loved she was.

I cannot go back in time to tell her that, but I can choose to live my life in a manner that allows for others to never go a day without knowing just how important and how very special they are to me.

Now, most days I retreat into the woods, where I am always reminded of how lucky I am to feel unhurried by the world around me or distracted by its countless storms. Yes, there have been many storms along my journey, but I have a better arsenal to fight them now.

Most days when faced with life on life's terms, I can handle it through epic simplicity—remembering my CORE Method:

C – Challenge (my goals)

O – Obstacles (the things that may stand in the way of progress toward my goals)

R – Reason (my why, my motivation)

E – Excuses (the false truths I tell myself)

After three slaps of the Snooze button, I laced up my hiking shoes and headed out the door and into my backyard. The yard is adjacent to a trail that leads to an overlook, the most beautiful landscape from which to watch the sun rise. The perfect place to practice surrendering.

Once again, on this peaceful summer morning, I surrendered her—my mother. I turned toward the sunrise, feeling its warmth across my face, just as I did on the morning I felt my mother go. Only now I could let go of all expectations. I whispered it all to the wind to be carried away so I could return to my home, to my family, a little lighter, a little softer, a little calmer.

I released my regrets, my resentments, my will, my alcoholism, my cancer, my disfigured chest, my inadequacies, my all...

I surrendered it all into the wind and emancipated myself from my suffering, allowing the freedom to face the world with epic simplicity, as light as a feather.

The Wind
by Valerie Walsh

The colors of the wind,
I imagine in my mind.
They take me to a place,
That's so often hard to find.

For some it whispers softly,
Speaking gently from a distance.
For me it's ever-present,
Demanding that I listen.

And when the breeze so graciously
Passes me with warmth across my face,
I imagine it must be Mother Nature,
Healing me with her embrace.
Whether the wind blows fierce or gently,
Is not something for me to foresee,
But when she speaks, I will listen,
To what she is saying to me.

Epilogue

With five years of sobriety and perspective at the time my story is being published, I no longer try to force my will upon people, places, or things. I've learned the importance of letting go of expectations. This was a most profound lesson, one taught to me through spending years placing such unfair notions on my very own mother, aching for her to show me a sign that she was finally at peace.

These days, my peace comes from daily practices because I am *far* from perfect and don't assume I am anywhere near achieving perfection while here on earth.

I still coach my CORE Fitness Method, which has also evolved into much more than just a physical fitness accountability group, and continues to grow. It is a group where not only can I can share my story and practices but others can share as well. CORE Fitness Method is now available in person and online so I am able to work with people from all over the world.

Since adding mental health advocate to my purpose in life, I have also had the honor of working with individuals and groups who know the importance of maintaining solid mental health through the power of exercise. I am proud to collaborate with professionals in the field, such as NAMI, as well as doctors and therapists.

I am just getting started with my CORE purpose in this life and look forward to sharing more with my readers—my peeps.

Photos

You've reached the photographs section of this book. If you're a reader like me, this is the part I tend to jump to, as it allows me to get to know the author. My one regret is that I have few pictures of my mother and me together; I wish I had taken more.

I chose these images to demonstrate the power of exercise, and how it can help in the complex battle against depression and anxiety. There were times when I was in the thick of it that I would look back at pictures of myself and see how happy I appeared, wondering if that girl would ever return again. Would she ever feel joy—or anything at all—again?

She returned. Stronger, wiser, and with a warrior heart.

If you're having more bad days than good, you'll return, too—and you don't have to do it alone. Please have the willingness to surrender and reach out for help. I thank God every day for placing the people, places, and things in my life that have enabled me to make peace with my past and reclaim my future.

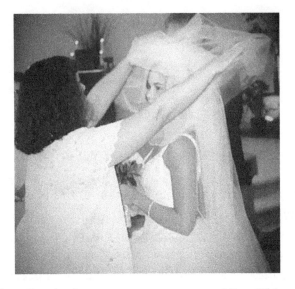

My mother, Sheryl, who gave me away at my wedding. This was a well-earned and proud moment for a special person who had taken on the responsibilities of both mother and father, raising her girls.
June 26, 1999

A sweet moment. My mother and me.
Summer, 1985

This is me completing the Mount Washington Auto Road Bicycle Climb. It's been called the ride of a lifetime at 7.6 miles, with an average grade of 12 percent, monstrous 18 percent extended parts, and a cherry-on-top finish at 22 percent!
August 20, 2016.

Ascending to the top of Mount Washington.

An appearance at one of the many adventure races I've participated in over the years.

Sasha, my best friend and hiking partner.
Fall, 2020

Sasha and me.
Summer 2021

A peaceful moment of surrender. Kaaterskill Falls, Catskills, New York. *Fall, 2021*

A serene moment captured while taking a break from road biking.
Fall, 2021

Here I am, doing what I love most: coaching the CORE Fitness Method.

Author Bio

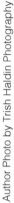

Author Photo by Trish Haldin Photography

VALERIE WALSH is a Nationally Certified Personal Trainer and Group Fitness Instructor, TRX Certified Trainer, 200 Hour YTT Graduate from Lotus Gardens Yoga School, P90X Certified Trainer, and Star Two Mad Dogg Athletics Spinning Instructor. She also coaches the CORE Fitness Method, a community-based group committed to improving the overall Physical and Spiritual CORE Fitness of its members.

For over twenty-five years Valerie has been dedicated to helping others achieve their physical fitness goals.

The suicide of her mother in 2013 prompted her to look a little deeper into paying attention to her own Spiritual Fitness, the CORE of herself, when she started experiencing bouts of depression and overwhelming anxiety. She sought answers and put the work in each day to not only focus on her physical fitness, but her Spiritual CORE Fitness as well.

Valerie has been married for over twenty years and is the mother of two. She understands what it is like to try to "juggle it all" while finding the time to make herself a priority. She has a passion, a fire in her soul, to help others find their way out of the chaos of life, learn from the shattered pieces of the past, and reclaim a peaceful future.

Learn more about how Coach Valerie can work with you to improve your Physical and Spiritual CORE Fitness and more about the CORE Fitness Method at www.valeriejwalsh.com.

You can also connect with Valerie and her CORE Peeps on Facebook: @corefitnessmethod and on Instagram @ valeriejwalshauthor.